**A prayerfully prepared collection
of fourteen Bible studies**

*May 18, 2020 —
Clarissa,
You are a great blessing!. Loves Gladys Ford*

**By: Gladys Goldsby Ford
Cover Design By: Kharis Courtney
Editor: Megan Mosher**

ABBA, FATHER

**Scripture quotations are from the
King James Version of the Bible.
All Greek and Hebrew definitions
are from the Strong's Exhaustive Concordance.**

You are welcome to copy portions of this book.
However, no portion is to be reproduced and sold.

TABLE OF CONTENTS

Page

- 4   Dedication
- 5   A Certain Rich Man
- 16   Blessed and Highly Favored
- 27   Cornelius the Centurion
- 33   His Loving-Kindness
- 47   If Any Man
- 50   Leah Was Her Name
- 70   Naaman the Sincere Syrian
- 85   Oh, God, Remember Me!
- 95   Pour Out Your Heart
- 107   Provoked to Prayer
- 120   The Centurion at Capernaum
- 125   The Cry of the Lord
- 139   The Dead Are To Be Buried
- 145   Thirty and Eight Years

DEDICATION

This book of Bible expositions was written to honor Jesus and to encourage those whose hearts cry, **"ABBA, FATHER."**

Jesus was filled with sorrow when He fell to the ground in Gethsemane and prayed:

Mark 14:36 ... Abba, Father, all things are possible unto thee. Take away this cup from me; Nevertheless, not what I will but what thou wilt.

The original word "Abba" was Aramaic before the Greek translation was made of the New Testament. Abba is a sacred name of God expressing deep adoration.

Apostle Paul, in the following two scriptures, used the term "Abba, Father" twice and associated it with the cry from our hearts.

Romans 8:14-15 For as many as are led by the Spirit of God, they are the sons of God. For ye have not received the spirit of bondage again to fear; but ye have received the Spirit of adoption, whereby we cry, Abba, Father.

Galatians 4:6 And because ye are sons, God hath sent forth the Spirit of his Son into your hearts, crying, Abba, Father.

May these studies bless you and enrich your understanding of God's word.

A CERTAIN RICH MAN and
A CERTAIN BEGGAR
with CERTAIN DESTINIES

Only the Gospel of Luke speaks of "<u>a certain rich man and a certain beggar</u>." Some believe that Jesus taught this story as a parable; however, a parable does not name an individual as Luke's narrative does. Lazarus the beggar is not to be confused with Lazarus the wealthy brother of Mary and Martha of Bethany.

Luke 16:19-21 There was <u>a certain rich man</u>, who was clothed in purple and fine linen, and fared sumptuously every day. And there was <u>a certain beggar</u>, named Lazarus, who was laid at his gate, full of sores, and desiring to be fed with the crumbs, which fell from the rich man's table; moreover, the dogs came and licked his sores.

What a contrast in human existence these few words reveal. Though rich men and beggars were common in Bible times, this specific rich man and beggar were used by Jesus to teach valuable truth. We are not told the source of the rich man's wealth or that his wealth had been gotten by corrupt means. Neither are we told the cause of the beggar's pitiful plight.

Because purple was considered a sign of royal opulence, the Roman soldiers placed a purple robe on Jesus to mock Him prior to the crucifixion. The rich man clothed himself in purple and fine linen every day in an open display of wealth. In contrast, Lazarus' robe had an unmistakable stench. The term, "full of sores" reveals the extent of his painful condition, which was without doubt irksome and repugnant.

It's been said that if you cannot lend a penny at least lend a hand. Lazarus, being laid at the rich man's gate, indicated that someone else had lent him a hand. That special someone was not afraid to touch this beggar.

Lazarus had accepted his fate without complaining about his misery while he begged for mercy. He was not expecting his existence to improve. But then a wonderful thing happened.

Luke 16:22 And it came to pass that the beggar died, and was carried by the angels into Abraham's bosom; the rich man also died, and was buried **...**

And "it came to pass" that the beggar did not remain a beggar and the rich man did not remain a rich man. Their destinies became irreversible at death just as ours will.

Souls exist separate from the body and do not die when the body does. Upon the physical death of Lazarus, he was carried, not by the charity of others, but on the wings of the angels of God. He was given an honored escort into the bosom of Abraham. "Bosom" is a Greek word (#2859) meaning, "a bay or creek." And then we are told what happened to the rich man after his physical body was buried.

Luke 16:23-24 And in hades he lifted up his eyes, being in torments, and seeth Abraham afar off, and Lazarus in his bosom. And he cried and said, Father Abraham, have mercy on me, and send Lazarus, that he may dip the tip of his finger in water, and cool my tongue; for I am tormented in this flame.

Hades (or hell) is the realm of the unsaved dead who are awaiting the white throne judgment. **(Revelation 20:11-15)** Souls there are conscious of lost opportunities and of their own hopelessness. They are aware of their absolute, permanent separation from God. They are in unspeakable torment.

The rich man's prayer to "send Lazarus" may have been an acknowledgement of his own now-pitiful existence where even temporary relief from his suffering would be better than none. He knew the judgment of God was irrevocable and dared not ask for deliverance. Lazarus had begged for crumbs; now the rich man begged for one drop of water.

Proverbs 21:13 Whoso stoppeth his ears at the cry of the poor, he also shall cry himself, but shall not be heard.

Abraham answered the rich man:
Luke 16:25 But Abraham said, Son, remember that thou in thy lifetime receivedst thy good things, and likewise Lazarus evil things; but now he is comforted, and thou art tormented.

Abraham graciously addressed the man as "son," even though he had forfeited all that could have been his as an heir of the kingdom of God. By Abraham's word we know that the now-dead rich man could remember his lifetime.

Notice that both Lazarus and the rich man "received" things in this life. While in this life, Godly people may receive evil things, whereas, in eternity they only receive good things. Likewise, wicked people may receive good things in this life but will receive only evil things after death.

Have you observed that some people seem to have the Midas touch, meaning that everything they touch turns to gold? Others appear to be in great adversity from the cradle to the grave. The important thing is not what people receive in this life, but what they do with what is received. Abraham was a great and rich man, but he was not consumed with earthly pleasure as the rich man was. Lazarus was consumed with oozing sores, reproach, and hunger but is now comforted and honored.

Abraham continued to answer the rich man:
Luke 16:26-27 And besides all this, between us and you there is a great gulf fixed, so that they who would pass from here to you cannot; neither can they pass to us, that would come from there.

:28 Then he said, I pray thee, therefore, father, that thou wouldest send him to my father's house (for I have five brethren) that he may testify unto them, lest they also come into this place of torment.

Acknowledging the spiritual condition of his living brothers, the rich man begged for their souls. We can only wonder at the number of times his five brothers passed Lazarus on their way to merriment in their brother's house.

Luke 16:29-31 Abraham saith unto him, They have Moses and the prophets; let them hear them. And he said, Nay, father Abraham; but if one went unto them from the dead, they will repent. And he said unto him, <u>If they hear not Moses and the prophets, neither will they be persuaded, though one rose from the dead</u>.

This was the rich man's third and final request and his third and final denial. No prayer request from hades is ever granted, and yet he attempted to dispute the undisputable with Abraham.

In the five verses that record the words of the rich man, he addressed Abraham as "father" three times. We aren't told when this man lived, but it's apparent that he never knew the reconciled Father-Son relationship Jesus came to accomplish.

Jesus spoke the following words to those who, like the rich man, had the Law of Moses and the prophets but who lacked a relationship with God:

Luke 13:28 There shall be weeping and gnashing of teeth, when ye shall see Abraham, and Isaac, and Jacob, and all the prophets, in the kingdom of God, and you yourselves thrust out.

Jesus spoke of the separation of sinners from the righteous. He said those who had done the work of the Father would be rewarded by inheriting the kingdom of God. Those who fail to serve Him as He desires, will hear Him say:

Matthew 25:41-42 ... Depart from me, ye cursed, into everlasting fire, prepared for the devil and his angels; For I was hungry, and ye gave me no food ...

The rich man hadn't given the beggar any actual food, only crumbs from beneath his table.

Psalm 49 bemoans the folly of those who are rich in this life and yet do not love God as they should and who are not prepared for eternity.

Psalm 49:17-20 For when he dieth he shall carry nothing away; his glory shall not descend after him, though while he lived he blessed his soul; and men will praise thee, when thou doest well to thyself. He shall go to the generation of his fathers; they shall never see light. Man that is in honor, and understandeth not, is like the beasts that perish.

In the closing statement, spoken by Abraham in our scripture study, he said, "If they will not hear Moses and the prophets, neither will they be persuaded, though one rose from the dead." We, too, have the word of Moses and the prophets. And more than that, we have the same spirit that raised Christ Jesus from the dead and have the entire Bible. How much more should we hear the voice of God?

What does "hear Moses and the prophets" mean?

The Bible has been called God's gracious self-disclosure. In it He bares His heart to feeble, fallen, finite man in an effort to gain the love and honor He desires and deserves.

Nineteen Old Testament books bear the name of prophets. Some are called minor prophets and others major prophets, referring only to the length of the writings and not to the content value. Moses, Elijah, and Hezekiah were prophets, although no books bear their names.

Here are some words from God's heart spoken by the prophets: Moses, Jeremiah, and Isaiah:

Deuteronomy 5:29 *Oh, that there were such a heart in them, that they would fear me, and keep all my commandments always, that it might be well with them and with their children forever!*

Deuteronomy 9:13 *... I have seen this people, and behold, it is a stiff-necked (obstinate, stubborn when in trouble) people.*

Jeremiah 2:32 *Can a maid forget her ornaments, or a bride her attire? Yet my people have forgotten me days without number.*

Jeremiah 24:7 *And I will give them a heart to know me, that I am the Lord, and they shall be my people, and I will be their God; for they shall return unto me with their whole heart.*

Jeremiah 31:33 *But this shall be the covenant that I will make with the house of Israel: After those days, saith the Lord, I will put my law in their inward parts, and write it in their hearts, and will be their God, and they shall be my people.*

Isaiah 1:18 *Come now, and let us reason together, saith the Lord: though your sins be as scarlet, they shall be as white as snow; though they be red like crimson, they shall be as wool.*

Isaiah 11:10 *And in that day there shall be a root of Jesse, who shall stand for an ensign of the peoples; to him shall the Gentiles seek, and his rest shall be glorious.*

Jews divide Old Testament writings into three collections called testimony books: the Law of Moses, the prophets, and the Psalms. This may be why Jesus was careful to say:

Luke 24:44 And he said unto them, These are the words which I spoke unto you, while I was yet with you, that all things must be fulfilled, which were written in <u>the law of Moses, and in the prophets, and in the psalms</u> concerning me.

The New Testament was written by people who heard Moses and the prophets. Many of the recorded words of Jesus were quotes from twenty-four books of the Old Testament. New Testament writers included over 250 Old

Testament quotations. An additional 1,000 quotes are less direct or are a composite of scriptures. The prophet Isaiah is quoted eighty-five times in the New Testament. The Apostle Paul, a Pharisee and son of a Pharisee quoted Old Testament prophets ninety-three times. The Gospel of Matthew, written by a Levite, quotes from forty-three Old Testament prophets.

Luke 24:25-26 Then said he (Jesus) unto them, O foolish ones, and slow of heart to believe all that the prophets have spoken! Ought not Christ to have suffered these things, and to have entered into his glory?

John 1:45 Philip findeth Nathanael, and saith unto him, We have found him, of whom Moses in the law, and the prophets, did write, Jesus of Nazareth, the son of Joseph.

Because Philip heard Moses and the prophets, he recognized the promised Messiah.

The church was established by hearing and believing the voice of the prophets.

In the Book of Acts, many verses proclaim the validity of Old Testament prophets. Among those are:

Acts 3:18 *(Peter speaking) But those things, which God before had shown by the mouth of all his prophets, that Christ should suffer, he hath so fulfilled.*

Acts 10:43 *(Peter speaking to the Gentiles in Cornelius' house) To him (Jesus) give all the prophets witness, that through his name whosoever believeth in him shall receive remission of sins.*

Acts 24:14 *(Paul speaking before Felix, the governor) But this I confess unto thee that, after the way that they call heresy, so worship I the God of my fathers, believing all things which are written in the law (of Moses) and the prophets ...*

The following scripture was spoken by Paul to the Jewish leaders after his arrival at Rome:

Acts 28:23-24 *And when they had appointed him a day, there came many to him into his lodging, to them he expounded and testified the kingdom of God, persuading them concerning Jesus, both <u>out of the law of Moses, and out of the prophets</u>, from morning till evening. And some believed the things which were spoken, and some believed not.*

Those of us living today who believe and endeavor to hear Moses and the prophets, will undoubtedly hear and know the heart of God.

The Gospel of Mark begins by quoting Malachi 3:1 from the Old Testament and acknowledging the prophets.

Mark 1:2 As it is written in the prophets, Behold, I send my messenger before thy face, who shall prepare thy way before thee.

Many who were blinded by religion failed to recognize the one standing in their midst.

Matthew 5:17 (Jesus said) Think not that I am come to destroy the law, or the prophets; I am not come to destroy, but to fulfill them.

By His sacrificial death on the cross, Jesus accomplished what the Law could not: the redemption of mankind.

BLESSED AND HIGHLY FAVORED

We are introduced to Mary, the mother of Jesus, in the genealogy listed in the first chapter of the Gospel of Matthew. The Gospel of Mark does not mention Mary by name; whereas the Gospel of John only speaks of her as being at His cross. This makes the detailed narrative recorded by Luke, the brother of Titus, even more valuable.

Luke, the only Gentile writer in the New Testament, also wrote The Acts of the Apostles. He addressed both of these writings to his friend Theophilus. Luke never knew Jesus during His earthly life. He received the Lord later under the ministry of Paul at Troas.

In Luke's opening chapter, we find Mary, a young twelve or possibly thirteen-year-old virgin of the tribe of Judah and of the lineage of David, espoused (Greek #3423 meaning, "betrothed or engaged") to Joseph.

The angel Gabriel was sent from God to inform this startled young virgin that she was to be the mother of the promised Messiah. Gabriel did not identify himself to her as he had to Zacharias earlier. Neither did she challenge his proclamation as Zacharias had challenged the angel's message to him.

The angel Gabriel greeted Mary with these words:
Luke 1:28 ... Hail, thou who art highly favored, the Lord is with thee; blessed art thou among women.

Quite naturally this young virgin was troubled by his greeting and wondered at its meaning.

Luke 1:30-33 And the angel said unto her, Fear not, Mary; for thou hast found favor with God. And, behold, thou shalt conceive in thy womb, and bring forth a son, and shalt call his name JESUS. He shall be called great, and shall be called the Son of the Highest; and the Lord God shall give unto him the throne of his father, David. And he shall reign over the house of Jacob forever; and of his kingdom there shall be no end.

It would be impossible to convey the gravity of this pronouncement to this unsuspecting young girl. She had been taught since her early childhood to expect the Messiah to come and redeem Israel. She could not have dreamed that her firstborn would be the promised Messiah and that He would suffer and die to redeem all of mankind.

NOTE: Scripture records when an angel speaks to man, his initial words are, "Fear not." This greeting changes to "Fear God" in Revelation 14:7 after the church is raptured prior to the hour of God's judgment.

Luke 1:34-35 Then said Mary unto the angel, How shall this be, seeing I know not a man? And the angel answered, and said unto her, The Holy Ghost shall come upon thee, and the power of the Highest shall overshadow thee; therefore also that holy thing which shall be born of thee shall be called the Son of God.

We are not told why Mary was chosen for such an appointment; however the words she spoke in reply to Gabriel's pronouncement revealed her heart. She resolutely replied:

Luke 1:38 And Mary said, Behold the handmaid of the Lord; be it unto me according to thy word. And the angel departed from her.

Following this discourse, Mary traveled to visit her cousin Elizabeth. Under the power of the Holy Ghost, Elizabeth proclaimed, "And blessed is she that believed; for there shall be a performance of those things which were told her from the Lord." And nestled among Mary's prophetic response were these words, "... from henceforth all generations shall call me blessed." **(Luke 1:48)**

This Mary, who was one of six New Testament women named Mary, was destined to live a life of perplexity stacked with unprecedented events. This "blessed and highly favored" young virgin would face much adversity and hardship as she became the catalyst for the Messiah's entry into the sphere of human existence. Being "great with child" and trekking by donkey and on foot some seventy fatiguing miles to Bethlehem is just one example of God not granting shortcuts in her life's experience. And, God may very well not grant shortcuts in your life's journey either.

The marriage of Joseph and Mary was blessed by Joseph's obedience to five God-given dreams and by Mary's compliance to God's directing the family through her husband as recorded in the first and second chapters of Matthew. God had spoken directly to Mary through the angel Gabriel prior to their marriage, however, now she would be directed by God through Joseph, the God-ordained head of their household.

God did not jolt her by a dream in the night saying, "Arise, and take the young child and his mother, and flee into Egypt, and be thou there until I bring thee word; for Herod will seek the young child to destroy him." **(Matthew 2:30)** But He did lay this disturbing news upon Joseph, the head of the family.

It's sad to say that perhaps a modern-day wife might have retorted, "Look Joe, you do what you have to do, but you are not taking <u>my</u> kid out in the night and fleeing to the heathen land of Egypt. God's not speaking that to me, and I can hear His voice as well as you!"

Without a doubt both Joseph and Mary learned later of Herod's slaughter of all the children two years old and younger following their departure from Bethlehem. Certainly they were shocked at such brutality and certainly they wondered.

Mary was the <u>only person</u> to be with Jesus from His conception and birth, throughout His life, His crucifixion, and His resurrection.

Interestingly, not one word spoken by Joseph is recorded. It seems that God intended for this special and chosen man to remain anonymous.

Later Joseph and Mary had a son whom they named Joseph, which must have been a fulfillment of their deep desire. Their children's names listed in **Matthew 13:55-56 and Mark 6:3** were: James, Joseph, Simon, and Judas (Jude) along with his unnamed sisters. Including Jesus, there was at least seven children in their household.

The last mention of this devout man, Joseph, is found in **Luke 2:41** where we are told he had taken his family to Jerusalem for the Passover when Jesus was twelve years old. It is believed that Joseph had already died by the time Jesus performed His first miracle at the wedding in Canaan. **(Matthew 2)** This beginning of Jesus' public ministry appears to also be the beginning of insight into His now dysfunctional family. Perhaps Joseph, no longer present, had been the stabilizing force in the family's structure.

   John 7:1-5 paints a disparaging picture of this dysfunctional family, by stating: "After these things Jesus walked in Galilee; for he would not walk in Judea, because the Jews sought to kill him. Now the Jews' feast of tabernacles was at hand. His brethren, therefore, said unto him, Depart from here, and go into Judea, that thy disciples also may see the works that thou doest. For there is no man that doeth anything in secret, and he himself seeketh to be known openly. If thou do these things, show thyself to the world. <u>For neither did his brethren believe in him.</u>"

These remarks were actually a blatantly cruel taunt spoken by His brothers who had no allegiance to Him whatsoever. We can envision and appreciate the quaking of Mary's heart at such insolent hostility knowing that their rejection of Jesus as the promised Messiah also meant they had rejected her account of His conception. How her heart must have been torn! Did she feel tormented and mocked by her own words, "... from henceforth all generations shall call me blessed?" Surely, this "blessed and highly favored" woman did not think of herself as being "blessed and highly favored" as she endured overwhelming heart-rending experiences without the support of her husband or her children. She must have fought to hold onto the words spoken by Gabriel decades before, as she faced the onslaught of contrary circumstances. And you may struggle to hang onto words spoken by God personally to you as you walk through circumstances that contradict your God-given expectations.

With her heart fused to her firstborn Son, this "blessed and highly favored" woman remained at the cross along with her sister, and Mary the wife of Clopas, and Mary Magdalene. **(John 19:25)** She did not recoil from His horrendous and repulsive appearance, which was then so marred that He did not appear to be human.

Gabriel had said He would be called the Son of the Highest and yet He was called Beelzebub (lord of the flies). Gabriel had said the Lord God would give unto Him the throne of His father, David, and yet He was given thirty-nine lashes and a cruel cross.

Mary wept in the deepest of agony as she witnessed the Roman soldiers pacing before Him like a pack of feral dogs. Did she recall the prophetic and puzzling words which Simeon had spoken to her, "Yea, a sword shall pierce through thy own soul also …?" **(Luke 2:35)**

What extreme anguish Mary experienced when she heard Him cry, "My God, my God, why hast thou forsaken me?" Did she also feel forsaken by God? **(Matthew 27:46)**

The following two scriptures plainly reveal that Jesus did not anticipate being abandoned by God. You, too, may experience unexpected events as you follow a course directed by God.

John 8:29 And he that sent me is with me. The Father hath not left me alone; for I do always those things which please him.

John 16:32 After saying that all of the disciples would leave him, Jesus stated, " … and yet I am not alone, because the Father is with me."

John was the only disciple who didn't flee this appalling scene. In the midst of His suffering, Jesus committed His mother to John's care. Tradition would have mandated Mary be placed with her next oldest son. This departure from tradition may be another indication of how dysfunctional this blessed and highly favored woman's family had become.

We weren't given any scripture to describe her emotions but we know she must have been shaken to the core of her being. The daunting reality of the cross contradicted her God-given expectations. She could not read the future chapters of her life's saga to know that God was performing His word to her and His perfect will. (And neither can you yours).

BEYOND THE CROSS

Beyond the cross, we read that "Mary, the mother of Jesus," and His brethren were praying in the upper room with His disciples. **(Acts 1:14)** Obviously, His brothers' hearts had been persuaded days after His resurrection when He "showed himself alive after His passion by many infallible proofs ..." **(Acts 1:3)** We can only imagine the exhilarating joy and relief Mary and her sons felt at being truly united at last.

Two of our Lord's half-brothers, James and Jude, were to each write epistles (or letters) which are included in our New Testament. The Epistle of James, the earliest written New Testament book, was written approximately A.D.45-

50. The Epistle of Jude, written between A.D.70-80, is among the last written.

James used the following salutation to begin his epistle, "James, a servant of God and of the Lord Jesus Christ" making it clear to all readers that he was a servant and was not boasting of being the Lord's half-brother. He referred to Jesus again in the opening verse of the second chapter by writing, "our Lord Jesus Christ, the Lord of glory." His epistle, written to Jewish believers, uses fluent easy language and is forceful and direct. He addressed the seriousness of the quality of life believers live before God and speaks twice of the "coming of the Lord" indicating it was immediately expected.

By all accounts, James was the head of the church at Jerusalem. He is mentioned prominently six times in three other New Testaments books. It is thought that he never traveled outside of Jerusalem.

His epistle recognized God as "Father" four times, representing the reconciled relationship Jesus accomplished by His death. Old Testament saints did not usually refer to God as "Father." We rejoice in this relationship as one of our privileges in Christ.

Church historians record the death of James by stoning at the demand of the Sanhedrin in A.D. 62.

Without any claim of worthiness, Jude began his epistle by identifying himself as, "Jude, the servant of Jesus

Christ, and brother of James." Though only containing 25 verses, Jude used the title name of "Jesus Christ" five times.

At the time of Jude's writing, the cycle of apostasy had already begun to besiege the church. Facing persecution from without and apostasy from within, Jude sternly and vividly warned believers to "earnestly contend for the faith."

At the time of Jude's writing, his brother James, Stephen, Peter, and Paul had already been martyred. The future of the church was unclear and seemed uncertain. Knowing this, Jude did not mince his sometimes scathing words or show concern for the absence of decorum.

He did, however, end his letter with perhaps one of the most eloquent crescendos found in scripture by proclaiming **(Jude :24-25)**, "Now unto him who is able to keep you from falling, and to present you faultless before the presence of his glory with exceeding joy, to the only wise God, our Savior, be glory and majesty, dominion and power, both now and ever. Amen."

CONCLUSION

God's promises to Mary have been performed, are being performed, and will be performed. And, Mary, blessed art thou among women!

One of the purposes of this lesson is to encourage the reader to recognize that no one has ever lived who understood his own life fully or understood the times in which he lived.

Much of God remains a mystery. We are indeed fortunate to have the Bible containing His gracious self-disclosure and to have His abiding presence.

We should always be mindful that the scriptures teach:
Luke 12:48 For unto whomsoever much is given, of him much shall be required.

CORNELIUS the CENTURION

Imagine a devout Roman centurion fearing the God of Israel during the days following the crucifixion of Jesus by another centurion. Cornelius of Caesarea was such a man.

The tenth chapter of The Acts of the Apostles identifies Cornelius as "A devout man, and one that feared God with all his house, who gave much alms to the people, and prayed to God always." **(Acts 10:2)**

God sent an angel to let him know that he was accepted by Him and that he should send for Peter, who would come and tell him what he ought to do. The angel could have told Cornelius himself, however, God had chosen to commit the "ministry of reconciliation" to men who had themselves been reconciled. **(2nd Corinthians 5:18)**

The angel called Cornelius by name and told him he was to send for Peter who was lodging in Joppa, another seaport town. Cornelius immediately called two household servants and a devout soldier and told them of his angelic visitation and sent them on their way. It is notable that the Roman centurion and his personal soldier were both devout men.

On the next day, while they journeyed, Peter was on the rooftop praying. God showed him three times in a vision that he was not to call anything common (unclean). This was the opposite of what Peter had been taught all his life, but without understanding what the vision meant, Peter knew God wanted him to change his thinking. God did not give Peter any time to question, quarrel, or analyze. When changing your life's course, He may not give much time for you to ponder either.

Acts 10:19-20 While Peter thought on the vision, the Spirit said unto him, Behold, three men seek thee. Arise, therefore, and get thee down, and go with them, doubting nothing; for I have sent them.

Some have said that Peter hadn't been teachable; but his actions proved he was. How did he feel when he opened the gate and found a Roman soldier standing there along with two Jewish servants? It would be an understatement to say he was stunned.

Peter had been at the cross of our Lord. He saw and heard firsthand the cruel taunts and brutal treatment Jesus endured from the Roman centurion and soldiers. He saw them bow their knees pretending to worship Him. He saw them spit on His face. Now he finds a Roman soldier standing at the gate asking him to come to the house of a centurion. Strange – really strange.

Even with vivid memories of the cross, Peter knew he must now obey God and "go with them, doubting nothing." Still not understanding what this rapidly unfolding drama was about, Peter had to ask the visitors:
Acts 10:21 ... What is the cause for which ye are come?

You yourself may be sent on an odd odyssey by God while not understanding what it's all about. Get up and go, dear one, doubting nothing.

They told him of Cornelius' love for God and His people and of how the angel had instructed him to send for him to "hear words of him." Peter invited the three men to spend the night. The change in Peter's thinking could not have been more apparent. Had God not directly instructed him, he would not have considered inviting a Roman soldier in the house and much less to spend the night. The next day, taking six brethren with him, he left for Caesarea along with the three men from Cornelius' house.

Four days had passed since the angel appeared to Cornelius when Peter arrived at his house. In the meantime, Cornelius had called together his kinsmen and near friends who were all eager to hear the words Peter would speak. Those four days must have seemed like four months. Wouldn't it be wonderful to summons your kinsmen and near friends to your house to hear the gospel and to receive the Holy Spirit? It may just happen.

Acts 10:25-26 As Peter was coming in, Cornelius met him, and fell down at his feet, and worshiped him. But Peter took him up, saying, Stand up; I myself also am a man.

Peter and the six men **(Acts 11:12)** who accompanied him must have been astounded at such a sight. What they saw was quite opposite of what was seen at the cross. Peter, and those with him, were surely dumbfounded to see a Roman centurion, who had command over one hundred soldiers, falling down on his knees to worship not only a man but one who was a Jew and a disciple of Jesus!

What would have happened had Peter received this man's worship? To say the least, God's purposes in his life would have been thwarted. He may have been struck down by God just as King Herod was **(Acts 12:23)** after people worshiped him as a god (also at Caesarea). And, truly, the faith of those present may have been horribly misguided.

Cornelius gave no thought of what he stood to lose by seeking truth from a Jew who believed Jesus to be the Messiah. He was serving under the Roman-made King Herod who was a Jew in name only. King Herod was ruthless and had even ordered the execution of two of his sons a few years prior. This so-called Jewish king had built many temples of pagan worship. One such temple was dedicated to the worship of the Emperor himself.

In contrast, Cornelius showed no hesitation or fear when it came to pursing the true Jehovah-God. The significance of this is hard to grasp. Truly, this man loved God. And, truly God knew it!

   1st Corinthians 8:3 But if any man love God, the same is known of him.

Cornelius told Peter all that the angel had said, and without offering any refreshments or time to rest, he added:

Acts 10:33-35 ... Now, therefore, are we all here present before God, to hear all things that are commanded thee of God. Then Peter opened his mouth, and said, Of a truth I perceive that God is no respecter of persons; but in every nation he that feareth him, and worketh righteousness, is accepted with him.

Peter may have been astonished himself by the words he spoke, because until the time of Christ, the Hebrew people were the only people who worshiped the one true Jehovah-God.

Cornelius, his kinsmen, and near friends believed the words spoken by Peter. While Peter was still speaking to them, they began to speak in tongues and to magnify God as he poured out the promised Holy Ghost upon them. **(Acts 10:44)**

Peter commanded them to be baptized in the name of the Lord. What a magnificent occasion this was! Then, Peter was asked to tarry a few days. Only God knows how many souls were eventually added by this blessed out pouring. Later, at Jerusalem, Peter was required to vindicate his ministry to these Gentiles. **Acts 11:1-18** details him relating the glorious event at the house of Cornelius. The major point of contention then was only that Peter had gone unto the uncircumcised and eaten with them. Talk about making an issue of a non-issue!

Acts 11:2-3 And when Peter was come up to Jerusalem, they that were of the circumcision contended with him, Saying, Thou wentest in to men uncircumcised, and dist eat with them.

Their religious mindsets did not comprehend the magnitude of Gentiles receiving the Holy Ghost and being welcomed into the family of God. They tripped over carnal trivia.

Peter's rebuttal convinced them that the whole matter was of God. Interestingly, he never mentioned the name Cornelius or the fact that he was a Roman centurion. Peter referred to Cornelius only as, "the man."
    Acts 11:12 Moreover, these six brethren accompanied me, and we entered into the man's house.

Just prior to Cornelius, his kinsman, and friends receiving the gift of the Holy Ghost, Peter declared:
    Acts 10:34-35 Then Peter opened his mouth, and said, Of a truth I perceive that God is no respecter of persons; but in every nation he that feareth him and worketh righteousness, is accepted with him.

Many times the religious mindset is limited by an "us four and no more" mentality that may exclude those who have been accepted by God.

HIS LOVING-KINDNESS

Daniel 11:32 Such as do wickedly against the covenant shall be corrupt by flatteries; but the people that do know their God shall be strong and do exploits, and they that understand among the people shall instruct many.

God's people must diligently apply their hearts to understanding His word and His ways; especially in the days in which we live. Overcomers must persevere in their faith by seeking God and focusing on understanding the things of God.

Notice the words "loving-kindness" and "earth" in the scripture below. We can better understand what the Spirit is saying by "loving-kindness" when we think of it as being God's offer of genuine friendship. Also, it's interesting to note the word "earth" in scripture many times is speaking of man's heart.

Jeremiah 9:23-24 Thus saith the Lord, Let not the wise man glory in his wisdom, neither let the mighty man glory in his might, let not the rich man glory in his riches, but let him that glorieth glory in this, that he <u>understandeth and knoweth me</u>, that I am the Lord who exerciseth loving-kindness, judgment, and righteousness in the earth; for in such things I delight, saith the Lord.

By these scriptures, God tells us plainly what He delights in. Our lifetimes are limited; so let's spend our lifetimes being concerned with the things that please and delight the Lord.

God declared that He is the Lord who exerciseth loving-kindness (He extends genuine friendship) then judgment (to purge all that offends His holiness) and righteousness (a pure reconciled standing before Him). He is saying that He exercises these things in the earth (or heart of man). Have you ever had the Potter's hand massage your earth (heart)? He does this first so He can then do the work of judgment (removing all things that offend); followed by His imputed righteousness.

We know from studying scripture that man is usually frightened when an angel appears. When Mary Magdalene and the other women arrived at His empty tomb, there was a great earthquake as the angel rolled away the stone and said to the women, "Fear not, for I know that ye seek Jesus, who was crucified." **(Mathew 28:5)** For those who are seeking Him today, His message is still, "Fear not."

God's desire for mankind is the same as it was before the foundation of the world. His desire is to have a people of His own who truly love Him and who accept His offer of genuine friendship or loving-kindness.

Romans 8:20 For the creature (mankind) was made subject to vanity, not willingly but by reason of him who hath subjected the same in hope.

God ordained man be subject to vanity (pride) in the hope that He would love the Creator more than the creature. This was the problem with Adam who loved the creature (Eve) more than the Creator God.

The first chapter of Romans has a lot to say about those who, after they knew God, chose to walk in the vanity of their minds, and, because of this, they were alienated from the life of God.

Romans 1:21, 24-25 Because, when they knew God, they glorified him not as God, neither were thankful, but became vain in their imaginations, and their foolish heart was darkened. (24-25) Wherefore, God also gave them up to uncleanness through the lusts of their own hearts, to dishonor their own bodies between themselves.

Consider the relation between the instructions given in the two following scriptures:
    John 3:19 And this is the condemnation, that light came into the world, and men loved darkness rather than light, because their deeds were evil.
    Romans 8:1 There is, therefore, now no condemnation to them who are in Christ Jesus, who walk not after the flesh, but after the Spirit.

The Holy Ghost will bring conviction of sin and judgment to come but never condemnation. If you are feeling condemnation, be assured that it's not coming from Father God. Ask Him to remove it and He will.

Genesis 5:24 Enoch walked with God, and he was not; for God took him.

Hebrews 5:11 By faith Enoch was translated that he should not see death, and was found not, because God had translated him; for before his translation he had this testimony, <u>that he pleased God</u>.

Every one of us has the hope of being translated (or raptured) when Jesus comes to take His bride away. But we must have the Enoch testimony: that we walked with God and were pleasing to Him. **(Genesis 5:24)**

Revelation 12:11 And they overcame him by the Blood of the Lamb and by the word of their testimony; and they loved not their lives unto the death.

We are told that Abraham walked with God and that Abraham believed God. Three scriptures say that Abraham was called God's friend. What an unspeakable honor and privilege to walk with God, to believe Him, and to be called His friend. **(2nd Chronicles 20:7, Isaiah 41:8, James 2:23)**

Jesus offered friendship to His disciples after Judas Iscariot had departed.

John 15:15 Henceforth, I call you not servants; for the servant knoweth not what his lord doeth: but I have called you friends; for all things that I have heard of my Father I have made known unto you.

John 16:12 I have many things to say unto you, but ye cannot bear them now.

Jesus spoke these words to His disciples after He had told them that He would be going away, that He would send the comforter, and that they would have persecution. His going away was incomprehensible to them, and the thought of it made them sorrowful. God wants His children to "grow-up" in Him so He can tell them His secrets and so He can share the longing and desires of His heart.

To better appreciate the nuggets He is going to present in this lesson, let's examine the words "friendship" and "enmity."

James 4:3-4 Ye ask, and receive not, because ye ask amiss, that you may consume it upon your lusts. Ye adulterers and adulteresses, know ye not that the friendship of the world is enmity with God.

The word "enmity" is the Greek word #2189 meaning, "hostile, hatred."

John 3:16 For God so loved the world, that he gave his only begotten Son, that whosoever believeth in him should not perish, but have everlasting life.

God loves a world created by Him and that world is returning enmity (hostile hatred) against Him. Have you ever had hostile hatred returned to you while you were demonstrating love and mercy?

The Bible speaks of "loving-kindness" thirty times. Twenty-three of those times are in Psalms, and King David wrote twenty-one of those. Here are some of what these Psalms declare about His loving-kindness:

119:88 His loving-kindness quickens us and brings us back to life.

63:3 His loving-kindness is better than life.

143:8 He causes us to hear his loving-kindness in the morning.

42:8 He commands his loving-kindness toward us in the daytime.

51:1 He blots out our transgression according to his loving-kindness.

How undeserved is His gracious loving-kindness. King David understood this. Although, during his adulthood King David sinned greatly, God had said while he was yet a shepherd boy that he was a man after His own heart. **(1st Samuel 13:14, Acts 13:22)**

We tend to associate the statement regarding David being a man after God's own heart with Psalm 51, the great psalm of deep repentance, which King David wrote after the prophet Nathan exposed his sin with Bathsheba and in the murder of faithful Uriah. But let's consider that King David's acknowledgment and repentance came only after he had been exposed.

Through this lesson, the Lord is going to show us something in the heart of King David that caused God to declare that he was a man after His own heart.

David was chosen to be king and anointed by God because, according to 1st Samuel, God looked upon his heart. Some of what God saw in David was that his heart overflowed with loving-kindness (genuine friendship) to others.

When the shepherd boy was first called to stand before King Saul, scripture says that David looked upon him and loved him greatly. **(1st Samuel 16:21)** And, as you know, that love was never returned. Until the end of his life, Saul returned enmity (hostile hatred) to David. And, yet, David constantly, consistently, and in every situation showed loving-kindness to Saul.

He served as Saul's armor bearer and, as such, was frequently in his presence. He never boasted, "I'm God's chosen. God has anointed me. I'll be king after you." David loved Saul and served him faithfully. However, even after he slew Goliath, Saul had to ask, "… whose son is this youth?" **(1st Samuel 17:55)** Saul failed to recognize he was being loved and served by someone extending loving-kindness. Isn't that the way of the world? And, sad to say, it's the way of some who are called by His name and yet who do not walk with Him as they should or love Him as He desires and as He deserves.

But Jonathan returned love to David. The moment they met their hearts were knit in true friendship. **(1st Samuel 18:1)** In direct contrast to Jonathan's love for David was Saul's enmity toward him.

When David received unsolicited praise from others, King Saul threw his javelin in an attempt to kill him. **(1st Samuel 18:10-11)** On another occasion, Saul threw his javelin at David so hard that it went through a wall. **(1st Samuel 19:10)** David had to flee through a window at night.

Once when Saul was told that David was sick on his bed, he commanded that he be brought to him on his sickbed so that he could kill him. Michal, Saul's daughter and also David's wife made a way of escape for him. **(1st Samuel 19:15)** But, because David was a man after God's own heart, he continued to show loving-kindness to Saul. David was not a vengeful man. He sought reconciliation. After all, he was a man after God's own heart.

David asked Jonathan to inquire of his father for him, and, when he did, Saul threw the javelin at him as well. **(1st Samuel 20:33)** David felt a deep sense of responsibility when eighty-five priests were slain because of their loyalty to him. **(Samuel 22:18)** His friend,

Jonathan, went to him and strengthened his hand in God. **(Samuel 23:16)** You know, it's good to have a friend who receives your offer of loving-kindness.

David had several choice opportunities to kill Saul, and each time he chose not to. Once, when Saul was asleep in a cave, David came in and cut off the end of his robe to signify that he could have killed him without mercy. **(1st Samuel 24:5)** Another time, Saul was sleeping in a trench, when David came upon him and took his spear and water vessel. It's curious that David's heart smote him for this. **(1st Samuel 26:12)**

All the way to **1st Samuel 26:18** David is still wondering why Saul is in hot pursuit when he has shown only kindness to him. He again asked three questions. "Why do you pursue me?" "What have I done?" and "What evil has been in my hand?" My, my, the heart of this man David.

In the first chapter of **2nd Samuel** we learn that David mourned the death of Saul as he had mourned the death of Jonathan. Keep in mind that all of these events took place before our shepherd boy was thirty years old.

   2nd Samuel 9:3 records David asking, "Is there not yet any of the house of Saul, that I may show the <u>kindness of God</u> unto him?"

When told of Jonathan's son, Mephibosheth, King David ordered that he be brought before him. He then restored all that had been his father's unto him and requested that he "eat at the king's table" throughout his lifetime. **(2nd Samuel 9:11)** This is a beautiful picture of God's mercy, grace, and loving-kindness.

1st Chronicles 19:2 and **2nd Samuel 10:2** record King David saying after the death of Hanun, the Ammonite's father, "I will show kindness unto Hanun." Yet his kindness was misinterpreted, and his men, who had been sent to bring condolences, were shamefully treated.

The **23rd chapter of 2nd Samuel** contains the eloquent account of King David's final and prophetic words and is the only scripture where he is named the "sweet psalmist of Israel." Scripture doesn't refer to anyone other than King David as being "sweet." It was noted earlier that the phrase "loving-kindness" is mentioned twenty-three times in the Book of Psalms and that twenty-one of these were written by King David.

2nd Samuel 15:26, 16:10-13, 2nd Samuel 24 all record the humble willingness of David to accept God's punishment for misdeeds.

2nd Samuel 24:17 And David spoke unto the Lord, when he saw the angel smote the people, and said, 'Lo, <u>I have sinned, and I have done wickedly</u>. But these sheep, what have they done?

1st Kings 2 records the instructions King David gave to his son Solomon while on his deathbed. He asked

Solomon to "show kindness" to the men who had helped him escape Absalom.

King David's heart was to show loving-kindness, just as the heart of God offers loving-kindness to all.

God's will and desire is to bless His people. The last words in Luke are:
Luke 24:50-53 And he led them out as far as Bethany; and he lifted up his hands, and blessed them. And it came to pass, while he blessed them, he was parted from them, and was carried up into heaven. And they worshiped him, and returned to Jerusalem with great joy; and were continually in the temple praising and blessing God. Amen.

Our Savior died with His arms open wide in a display of ultimate loving-kindness. He said, "Father, forgive them; for they know not what they do." **(Luke 23:34)** He could have added, "But You know what You are doing through Me for all mankind. You are extending full pardon and reconciliation. You are offering loving-kindness to all."

The second chapter of Ephesians tells us that we had been aliens and strangers and that we had had no hope and had been without God in the world. What a sorry state to be in. It goes on to say that Jesus is our peace and that He has abolished the <u>enmity</u> (hostile hatred) that <u>was</u> between God and man.

In Luke, we find another scripture that contrasts "friends" and "enmity."

Luke 23:11-12 And Herod, with his men of war, treated him with contempt, and mocked him, and arrayed him in a gorgeous robe, and sent him again to Pilate. And the same day Pilate and Herod were made <u>friends</u> together; for before they were at <u>enmity</u> between themselves.

Sequence in scripture can be important. There are eight sins listed in Revelation 21:8 that condemn people before God, and the first of these is what will be emphasized in our lesson.

Revelation 21:8 But the <u>fearful</u>, and unbelieving, and the abominable, and murderers, and fornicators, and sorcerers, and idolaters, and all liars, shall have their part in the lake which burneth with fire and brimstone, which is the second death.

"But the <u>fearful</u> …" are those who are afraid to come into His presence even knowing that He has made peace with them through the Blood of His Lamb, even knowing His arms are outstretched still, and that His loving-kindness is extended to all. Those who know this and remain fearful are sinning greatly; not trusting His grace and mercy.

Being fearful defrauds Jesus of His reward. God promised Jesus, before the foundation of the world, that His Blood would open a new and living way for even the vilest of sinner to be cleansed and fully reconciled. **(1st Peter 1:20-21)** Scripture tells us plainly that <u>He despised the shame of the cross</u>. Yet, He endured the contradiction of sinners against Himself **(Hebrews 12:2-3)** that we might be <u>unashamed</u> and blameless before the Father.

The story of Queen Vashti is recorded in one of the only two Bible books (Esther and Song of Solomon) that does not mention the name of God; not even a pronoun. But this book does contain rich spiritual truths and applications. This story is found in the Book of Esther and tells of Queen Vashti's refusal to respond when summoned by the king to come into his presence. Therefore, Queen Vashti is banished, her estate given to another, and she then vanished after losing all.

We, too, have been summoned to the presence of the King. His word to us is, "Fear not." He is waiting with arms open wide.

Because of the sins of envy and pride, Cain was banished from the presence of the Lord. He even said, "My punishment is more than I can bear." **(Genesis 4:13)**

Surely you do not want to be banished from the presence of the King Eternal.

Scripture says that the wages of sin is death. Jesus was paid the wages for our sin and shame that He might reconcile us to God. And His reward is presenting you in the presence of God. Do not defraud Him of His reward.

Do not return the javelin to His gracious offer of loving-kindness.

God does not judge as we judge. A woman heard the Lord say, "Behold, my faithful one." She felt she had been anything but faithful in her walk. She responded, "Lord, why do you call me faithful? You know I am not faithful. You know I have failed you over and over." And the Lord lovingly replied, "I say you are my faithful one because, when you fail, you are faithful in returning to Me."

If you have neglected coming into His presence, if you have not received His offer of loving-kindness, or if you feel you have fallen short, return to Him who died with His arms open wide, and He will judge you as faithful in returning. Take your place around His throne and not among the fearful in the lake of fire.

IF ANY MAN

Behold, I stand at the door, and knock; **If any man** hear my voice, and open the door, I will come onto him, and will sup with him, and he with me.
Revelation 3:20

If any man will come after me, let him deny himself, and take up his cross, and follow me.
Matthew 16:24

If any man have ears to hear, let him hear.
Mark 4:23

If any man desire to be first, the same shall be last of all, and servant of all.
Mark 9:35

I am the living bread that came down from heaven; **If any man** eat of this bread, he shall live forever ...
John 6:51

If any man will do his will, he shall know of the doctrine, whether it be of God ...
John 7:17

... **if any man** thirst, let him come unto me, and drink.
John 7: 37

I am the door; by me **if any man** enter in, he shall be saved, and shall go in and out, and find pasture.
John 10:9

If any man serve me, let him follow me; and where I am there shall also my servant be; **if any man** serve me, him will my Father honor. John 12:26

But **if any man** love God, the same is known of him.
1st Corinthians 8:3

Therefore, **if any man** be in Christ, he is a new creature (creation); old things are passed away; behold, all things are become new.
2nd Corinthians 5:17

... **If any man** preach any other gospel unto you than that ye have received, let him be accursed.
Galatians 1:9

Now the just shall live by faith; but **if any man** draw back, my soul shall have no pleasure in him.
Hebrews 10:38

If any man among you seem to be religious, and bridleth not his tongue, but deceiveth his own heart, this man's religion is in vain.
James 1:26

... And **if any man** sin, we have an advocate with the Father, Jesus Christ the righteous; and he is the

propitiation (Greek word #2434 meaning, "atonement") for our sins, and not for our sins only, but also for the sins of the whole world.
1st John 2:1-2

And **if any man** shall take away from the words of the book of this prophecy, God shall take away his part out of the book of life, and out of the Holy City, and from the things written in this book.
Revelation 22:19

LEAH WAS HER NAME
She Was Cheated, Hated, Envied, and Honored

When we study the word of God and examine the lives of people it portrays, we should keep in mind what Paul wrote in Romans 15:4, "For whatever things were written in earlier times were written for our learning, that we, through patience and comfort of the scriptures, might have hope." This study was researched and composed that you might have patience, comfort, and hope in God.

It is estimated that the people we will read about lived between 300 and 500 years before the giving of the law. Without having the written law of God and without the indwelling Spirit of God, their characters should not be judged by those who do.

NOTE: All scripture verses are from Genesis.

Our study begins with **Genesis 29:1**, which says, "And Jacob went on his journey, and came into the land of the people of the east."

Jacob had followed his mother's advice by disguising himself as his brother, Esau, in order to deceive his father, Isaac, into bestowing the birthright of the firstborn upon him.

Jacob also embarked on his journey at the suggestion of his mother, Rebekah, in order to escape the wrath of

Esau and to seek out a bride for himself from her kindred. Neither Rebekah nor Jacob knew that his journey would last twenty years and that they would not see each other again in this life.

Jacob traveled to the land of Haran where he met shepherds tending their flocks near a well. He was delighted when told that they knew Laban, his mother's brother, and that he was well. He was further delighted when the "beautiful and well favored" young Rachel, daughter of Laban, arrived to water her father's lambs. Rachel may have only been nine years old at that time.

Jacob rolled the stone from the well's mouth and watered Laban's flock. He then kissed Rachel in a kinship fashion, lifted up his voice, and wept at his good fortune. Rachel ran to tell the good tidings to her father who then ran to greet his new-found nephew, Jacob.

Jacob lived with and worked for Laban for one month without making his true mission known. When Laban asked him what he would like to be paid, Jacob, not having a dowry, made an expensive offer.

29:16-18 And Laban had two daughters: the name of the elder was Leah, and the name of the younger was Rachel. Leah was tender-eyed **but** Rachel was beautiful and well-favored. And Jacob loved Rachel; and said, I will serve thee seven years for Rachel, thy <u>younger</u> daughter.

Jacob made it clear he was bargaining for the younger daughter, Rachel. Laban then made it clear that he understood who and what they agreed upon.

29:20 And Jacob served seven years for Rachel; and they seemed unto him but a few days, for the love that he had for her.

How Jacob's heart must have raced during those seven years of labor without pay as he saw Rachel day by day. And surely, Rachel's eyes must have sparkled as she observed his adoration.

Jacob then asked Laban for his agreed upon wife. Laban gathered the men of Haran and made a great evening wedding feast. Under the cover of darkness and under the veil of deception, Laban presented the tender-eyed Leah to Jacob.

Jacob had earlier disguised himself as his fraternal twin brother, Esau, in order to deceive his father, Isaac, whose eyesight had failed. The deceived Isaac then pronounced the blessing of the firstborn on Jacob.

Seven years after Jacob's agreement with Laban, he began to reap a costly harvest for the deceitful seeds he had sown previously when he deceived his father and cheated his brother.

29:25 And it came to pass that, in the morning, behold, it was Leah: and he (Jacob) said to Laban, What is this thou hast done unto me? Did not I serve thee for Rachel? Wherefore then hast thou beguiled (Hebrew #7411 meaning, "deceived, betrayed") me?

Laban justified his treachery by explaining that in the country of Haran it was customary to give the firstborn in marriage before a younger sibling. Undoubtedly he could have made this custom known at any time before or during the seven years that Jacob served him without wages.

We are not given insight to the emotions of Jacob's undesired bride. But we do know that Leah had no choice. She obeyed her father and submitted herself to Jacob. Surely this young bride had dreamed of her wedding night and had longed to become one with her husband. This would not be the last time her dreams would not be realized. And surely she was painfully aware of the deception of her father and of Jacob's disappointment. The Hebrew (#3812) name "Leah," means "weary." Leah would become very weary before her earthly journey ended.

Laban, ever mindful of making a profit, then suggested that Jacob serve him another seven years for his younger daughter Rachel. Laban had cleverly used Rachel's outward beauty to dispose of his older tender-eyed daughter. This entire scenario has the DNA of manipulation. However, we will learn that God had His hand in it all.

At Laban's suggestion, Jacob fulfilled Leah's first week of marriage before taking his beloved Rachel as his second wife, thus setting the scene for heart-rending, dysfunctional family dynamics. This family portrait will not produce a Norman Rockwell painting.

29:30-31 And he went in also unto Rachel, and he loved <u>also</u> Rachel more than Leah, and served with him (Laban) yet seven other years. And <u>when the Lord saw that Leah was hated</u>, he opened her womb: but Rachel was barren.

By the use of the plural adverb "also," scripture is revealing that Jacob did love Leah. Notice that when the Lord saw that Leah was hated, he took action and comforted her by opening her womb while Rachel remained barren.

God wasn't alone in seeing that Leah was hated. Beyond doubt, Leah knew she was hated just as she knew her life's circumstance was not her own doing. The hate transmitted to Leah was not emitted by Jacob.

Verse 31 contains the first mention of our ever-present God in this unfolding narrative of lives mysteriously intertwined to accomplish His will and purpose.

God knew that what began as a forced marriage, through His divine intervention, would result in a majestic mosaic for His glory.

29:32-35 And Leah conceived and bore a son, and she called his name Reuben (a son); for she said, Surely the Lord hath looked upon my affliction; now therefore my husband will love me. And she conceived again and bore a son; and said, Because the Lord hath heard that I was hated, he hath therefore given me this son also: and she called his name Simeon (hearing). And she conceived again, and bore a son; and said, Now this time will my husband become attached (be joined) unto me, because I have borne him three sons: therefore was his name called Levi (joined, attached). And she conceived again, and bore a son: and she said, Now will I praise the Lord: therefore she called his name Judah (praise); and ceased (left off) bearing.

Leah did not need twenty-twenty vision to see what was going on around her. By her own words, we learn that Leah's expectation was in the Lord, that she knew she was afflicted, that her husband didn't love her as he should, that God and she both knew she was hated, that her desire was to be joined as one with her husband, and that she gave praise to God alone.

Chapter 30 begins with Rachel's intense escalation of her efforts to gain tribal dominance over her sister.

30:1-2 And when Rachel saw that she bore Jacob no children, Rachel <u>envied her sister</u>; and said unto Jacob, Give me children or else I die. And Jacob's anger was kindled against Rachel: and he said, Am I in God's stead, who hath withheld from thee the fruit of the womb?

Rachel's envy for Leah caused her to hate her too. Her demand of Jacob to "give me children or else I die," is almost a foreshadowing of the bitter words she spoke years later while dying in childbirth. **(Genesis 35:18)**

Jacob rightfully acknowledged that God was responsible for her childlessness without placing blame on anyone. Notice that "Jacob's anger was <u>kindled</u> against Rachel." Fire cannot be kindled unless embers are already smoldering. The fire of Jacob's anger toward Rachel was already burning before she stoked it with her envy-driven demand.

The Bible's first mention of someone being hated is found in **Genesis 27:41** where we are told that Esau hated his brother Jacob. Jacob knew what it was to be hated. He knew that he was hated for something he had done, and he knew that Leah was hated for something she did not cause and could not change.

30:3-6 And she (Rachel) said, Behold my maid, Bilhah; go in unto her, and she shall bear upon my knees, that I may also have children by her. And she gave him Bilhah, her handmaid, as his wife; and Jacob went in unto her. And Bilhah conceived, and bore Jacob a son. And Rachel said, God hath judged me, and hath also heard my voice, and hath given me a son: therefore called she his name Dan (judging).

In stating her plan, Rachel said she desired her maid to have "children" (not just one child) by Jacob. It seems that, by the birth of Dan, she felt God had justified her.

30:7-8 And Bilhah, Rachel's maid, conceived again, and bore Jacob a second son. And Rachel said, with great wrestlings have I wrestled with my sister, and I have prevailed: and she called his name Naphtali (wrestling).

This unfortunate competition had begun before Jacob arrived at the well. Rachel increased its momentum as her efforts gained traction by Bilhah producing two additional sons for Jacob.

From the beginning, Rachel had made their lives a contest. It wasn't a contest for Jacob's love. She already had that. It was a contest for dominance.

Rachel said that she "wrestled with my sister." The noun "wrestle" means to struggle hand to hand to gain dominance. It was Rachel who had been doing the wrestling up until now.

30:9-13 When Leah saw that she had ceased (left off) bearing, she took Zilpah, her maid, and gave her Jacob as his wife. And Zilpah, Leah's maid, bore Jacob a son. And Leah said, A troop cometh (Good fortune!) And she called his name Gad (a troop). And Zilpah, Leah's maid, bore Jacob a second son. And Leah said, Happy am I, for the daughters will call me blessed: and she called his name Asher (happy).

Asher was the eighth of what would become the twelve sons of Jacob.

Leah's firstborn son, Reuben was perhaps seven years old when he found mandrakes which he brought to his mother. **(30:14)** Mandrakes were thought to be something of an aphrodisiac producing fertility plant root. Rachel asked to be given the mandrakes. In verse 15 Leah responded by saying, "Is it a small matter that thou hast taken my husband? And wouldest thou take away my son's mandrakes also?"

This is the third of five times Leah referred to Jacob as, "my husband," a term never recorded as used by her sister. Rachel offered Jacob to Leah for the night in exchange for the mandrakes. Leah gladly accepted Rachel's self-serving offer. Note that possession of the mandrakes never produced fertility for Rachel. But a night with Jacob did produce yet another son for Jacob and Leah.

30:17-18 And God hearkened unto Leah, and she conceived, and bore Jacob a fifth son. And Leah said, God hath given me my hire, because I have given my maiden to my husband: and she called his name Issachar (hire).

30:19-21 And Leah conceived again, and bore Jacob the sixth son. And Leah said, God hath endued me with a good dowry; now will my husband dwell with me, because I have borne him six sons: and she called his name Zebulun (dwelling). And afterwards she bore a daughter, and called her name Dinah (judgment.)

With these births, Leah's childbearing ended.

30:22-24 And God remembered Rachel, and God harkened unto her, and opened her womb. And she conceived, and bore a son; and said, God hath taken away my reproach: And she called his name Joseph (adding) and said, The Lord shall add to me another son.

In **Chapter 31** Jacob discussed Laban's unfair treatment with Leah and Rachel. The three agreed that going to the land of Jacob's kindred was in their mutual best interest.

Jacob gathered all his goods in preparation to flee as Rachel took advantage of an opportunity to take something she desired which belonged to her father, Laban.

31:19 And Laban went to shear his sheep: and <u>Rachel had stolen the images</u> that were her father's.

Notice that Rachel stole more than one image or idol. Much speculation has been put forth as to what her motivation was in stealing her father's images. History reveals that whoever was in possession of the family's idols was considered the legitimate heir to all family property. This could possibly be an example of Rachel's attempting to usurp heirship over both her father and her sister.

Laban was told on the third day after their departure that Jacob had fled along with his family and all that he had. Laban took men with him and pursued after them seven days. Interestingly enough, God then spoke to Laban in a night dream warning him "not to speak to Jacob either good or bad."

Laban caught up with Jacob and asked, as though he was Jacob's victim, "What hast thou done, that thou hast stolen away unawares to me, and carried away my daughters, as captives taken with the sword?" **(31:26)**

Notice that the beginning words of Laban are the exact words Jacob had said to him years before upon discovering the secret bride-swap. Jacob's question then was, "What is this thou hast done unto me?" Now Laban launched into a lengthy tirade describing how personally offended he was at their stealing away while quoting God's warning for him not to speak either good or bad to Jacob. Yep, the words of a deceiver are always strange. He further stated how offended he was to have lost his idols also. Without knowing Rachel was the thief, Jacob responded with surprise that Laban's "little g gods" had been stolen. He declared that the person who had done this deed should die.

Laban searched Jacob's tent, Leah's tent, Bilhah's tent, and Zilpah's tent before entering Rachel's. Being last in the search gave her time to devise strategy in her grand, reoccurring, insidious theme for dominance over her perceived nemesis Leah.

Rachel had placed the images in a camel's saddle and sat upon it. Hunkered down on the contraband, she must have looked like a hen sitting on a lumpy nest. She deceived her father into thinking "the custom of women" was upon her and, therefore, she must remain anchored. Knowing the severity of her crime, and the pronounced death judgment of her husband, kept her affixed upon her trophies.

A heated dispute between Laban and Jacob erupted. Jacob reminded Laban twice that he had served him twenty years (seven years for each wife and six years for cattle and sheep). He pointed out that the God of his fathers had seen his affliction and the labor of his hands, and had rebuked him in a dream. Jacob told him that if it had not have been for the fear of the God of his forefathers, he would have sent him away empty.

Audaciously, Laban asserted that Leah, Rachel, their children, and all their flocks were his. He stated his case skillfully framing himself as the loser and a victim of Jacob.

Here is a major key to understanding the rationale of Laban. Having had the images of his "little g gods" stolen, he had no way of declaring he was the rightful land heir. This may have been why he attempted to reclaim his daughters and the possessions of their husband.

Laban declared all that he lost and what he hoped to gain as his sole possession—the land! He struck up a land boundary deal with Jacob to ensure its possession. They pledged not to cross boundaries to harm one another. **(31:44-52)**

31:53-54 (Laban concluded the pledge) The God of Abraham, and the God of Nahor, the God of their father, judge between us. And Jacob swore by the fear of his father, Isaac. Then Jacob offered sacrifice upon the mount, and called his brethren to eat bread: and they did eat bread, and tarried all night in the mount.

Jacob's sincerity showed through his actions. The agreement was made, an oath sworn, a sacrifice made to God, and a hearty meal was shared.

We are not told what became of the stolen idols. Perhaps Rachel thought they were of no value once the land boundaries were set. Or possibly she disposed of them when in **Genesis 35:4** Jacob commanded his household to put away "all the foreign gods which were in their hands." At that time Jacob secretly hid all of the foreign "little g gods" under an oak by Shechem.

Chapter 35:16-20 And as they journeyed from Bethel; and there was but a little way to come to Ephrath: and Rachel travailed, and she had hard labor. And it came to pass, when she was in hard labor, that the midwife said unto her, Fear not; thou shalt have this son also. And it came to pass, as her soul was in departing (for she died), that she called his name Benoni (the son of my sorrow): but his father called him Benjamin. And Rachel died, and was buried in the way to Ephrath, which is Bethlehem. And Jacob set a pillar upon her grave: that is the pillar of Rachel's grave unto this day.

It is evident that the dying Rachel spoke anguished bitter words from her heart. Her death may have been even more tragic for her newborn son had she succeeded in naming him Benoni (the son of my sorrow).

Jacob's daughter and other sons were named by his wives as a reflection of their own feelings. Benjamin (son of my right hand) was the only child named by Jacob.

It seems strange that there is no mention of mourning for Rachel. Her death and burial are stated as a matter of fact as Jacob as his entourage continued their journey.

Chapters 48-49 record the death of Jacob approximately twenty years later in the land of Goshen in Egypt.

48:1-2 And it came to pass after these things, that one told Joseph, Behold, thy father is sick: and he took with him his two sons, Manasseh and Ephraim. And one told Jacob, and said, Behold, thy son, Joseph, cometh unto thee; and Israel strengthened himself, and sat upon his bed.

Jacob reviewed with Joseph the promises God had spoken to him at Luz (Bethel). Jacob then blessed

Joseph's two sons born to him in Egypt, guaranteeing Joseph a double portion of the inheritance.

In **Chapter 49: verses 1-27**, Jacob pronounced his assessment of the virtues and short comings of each of his twelve sons. In verse 28 he gave specific instructions to be buried in the cave where his fathers were buried.

The Cave of the Patriarchs, the world's most ancient Jewish site, is located about 19 miles south of Jerusalem in Hebron. Abraham purchased the field where the cave is located as a burial place 3,700 years ago. Approximately 2,000 years ago, Herod, the Jewish-by-birth-only, king of Judea, built a massive mausoleum over the cave as a gathering place and a place of prayers for Jews. The shrine is today occupied by Muslims. Jews are only allowed in certain areas and are not permitted past the seventieth step.

49:28-31 All these are the twelve tribes of Israel (Jacob): and this is that which their father spoke unto them, and blessed them; every one, according to his blessing, he blessed them. And he charged them, and said unto them, I am to be gathered unto my people: bury me with my fathers in the cave that is in the field of Ephron, the Hittite, In the cave that is in the field of Machpelah, which is before Mamre, in the land of Canaan, which Abraham bought with the field of Ephron, the Hittite, for a possession of a burying place. There they buried Abraham and Sarah, his wife; there they buried Isaac and Rebekah, his wife; and there I buried **LEAH.**

Leah was the last recorded word spoken by Jacob.

Leah was cheated.

Leah was hated.

Leah was envied.

Leah is still being honored.

TWO SONS OF JACOB and LEAH

The tribe of Levi came from the loins of Jacob and the womb of Leah.

Exodus 32:26 (After finding the people worshiping the golden calf) Then Moses stood in the gate of the camp, and said, Who is on the Lord's side? Let him come unto me. And <u>all the sons of Levi</u> gathered themselves together unto him.

The tribe of Levi was the ONLY tribe not to worship the golden calf. Moses and both his parents were of the tribe of Levi.

The tribe of Levi served the sanctuary during the forty-year wandering. Because of their zeal for Jehovah-God, this tribe was chosen to bear the Ark of the Covenant.

Deuteronomy 10:8-9 At that time the Lord set apart the tribe of Levi, to bear the ark of the covenant of the Lord, to stand before the Lord to minister unto him, and to bless in his name, unto this day. Wherefore Levi hath no part or inheritance with his brethren; the Lord is his inheritance, according as the Lord thy God promised him.

The beginning of the Levitical priesthood

Deuteronomy 18:5 For the Lord thy God hath chosen him (Levi) out of all thy tribes, to stand to minister in the name of the Lord, him and his sons forever.

Deuteronomy 31:9 And Moses wrote the law, and delivered it unto the priests, <u>the sons of Levi</u>, who bore the ark of the covenant of the Lord ...

Joshua 18:7 (Joshua speaking) But the Levites have no portion among you; for the priesthood of the Lord is their inheritance.

The tribe of Levi was the ONLY tribe not to receive a land allotment.

The tribe of Levi came from the loins of Jacob and the womb of Leah.

The sons of Korah were of the tribe of Levi.

The descendants of Korah, known as the sons of Korah, did not participate in the rebellion against Moses. Afterwards, this tribe rose to eminence in the Levitical order. What is referred to as, "the sons of Korah," was a family of Levite singers who sang and wrote the following eleven psalms:

Psalm 42, 44, 45, 46, 47, 48, 49, 84, 85, 87, and 88

These psalms are characterized by a profound gratitude for the holiness and mercy of God. They are often poetic expressing utter dependence upon God alone. Is it any wonder that they are among the most favored and most quoted of the 150 psalms?

The tribe of Judah came from the loins of Jacob and the womb of Leah.

In Exodus 31:1-3, the Lord told Moses that he had called Bezalel (Bez-a-lel), a great-grandson of Judah, and had "filled him with the Spirit of God, in wisdom, and in understanding, and in knowledge, and in all manner of workmanship, to design skillful works, to work in gold, and in silver, and in bronze, and in cutting stones …"

Here is a partial list of items Bezalel crafted and over-laid with pure gold: the Ark of the Covenant, the mercy seat, two angels, table for the showbread, table vessels, spoons, bowls, seven lampstands, altar for burnt offerings, and all vessels for the altar. In addition, he made the holy anointing oil, the pure incense of sweet spices.

Bezalel came from the tribe of Judah which came from the loins of Jacob and the womb of Leah

All twelve spies sent by Moses into the land of Canaan brought back true reports. Even though God said that ten of the twelve spies brought back an evil report because they failed to trust Him. **(Numbers 13:32)** Caleb believed God and encouraged to people to trust God. Caleb was of the tribe of Judah, the only tribe whose land inheritance was determined by God prior to the invasion and conquest of Canaan. Their land allotment was far larger than any other tribe, covering 2,300 square miles.

Caleb was of the tribe of Judah.

King David was of the tribe of Judah.

Elizabeth, the mother of John the Baptist, was of the tribe of Judah.
Both Joseph and Mary, the mother of God, were of the tribe of Judah.

Revelation 5:5 identifies Jesus, as the Lion of the tribe of Judah.

<u>**Caleb, King David, Elizabeth, Joseph, Mary, and Jesus came from the loins of Jacob and the womb of Leah.**</u>

NAAMAN the SINCERE SYRIAN
2nd Kings 5:

Throughout recorded history, our God, the Creator of all things seen and unseen, has moved providentially at His will. We also know that the Bible records many events of great magnitude in the lives of individuals as though they were mere happenstance.

One of these events is recorded in **2nd Kings 5** where an unusual and seemingly unfortunate circumstance occurred in the life of a young unnamed captive Hebrew slave girl, and her master, Naaman, the supreme commander of the Syrian army.

Naaman was the recipient of extraordinary grace. The name, Naaman, was common in ancient Syria and means "gracious, fair, pleasantness." Perhaps by examining the scriptures concerning him, you will conclude that he was indeed gracious, fair, and pleasant.

2nd Kings 5:1 Now Naaman, captain of the host of the king of Syria, was a great man with his master, and honorable, because by him the Lord had given deliverance unto Syria; he was also a mighty man in valor, <u>but he was a leper.</u>

Rarely is a mere man praised in the Holy word of God, but Naaman was recognized as "a great man with his master, and honorable." Though in the midst of great honor, he was also a man of great affliction. God allowed the disease of Leprosy to reduce this mighty man of valor to a pitiful hopeless state. Even a slave would not have traded places with him.

Note: The leprosy spoken of in the Bible disfigured its victims but didn't cripple or disable them as modern day leprosy (Hansen's disease).

5:2 And the Syrians had gone out by companies, and had brought away captive out of the land of Israel a little (Hebrew #6996, meaning "young") maid; and she waited on Naaman's wife.

The Syrians captured this young Hebrew girl while conducting a night raid into Israel. The Hebrew word "little" literally means "young" and doesn't refer to her size. She was providentially catapulted into an undesirable circumstance in order that God could intervene through her to work a miracle. No one would desire to be stolen away from his or her family and country to live as a slave among a foreign enemy. However, she became obedient to her new role as servant to Naaman's wife. We are not told that the difficult life of this unnamed child-slave changed even after God used her in an extraordinary way.

5:3 And she said to her mistress, would to God my lord were with the prophet who is in Samaria! For he would cure him of his leprosy.

With no thought of being freed herself, she longed for her captor to be freed from this hideous disease. She had unequivocal faith that God would use His prophet Elisha to heal her master. Surely her faith was given to her by God to serve His purposes. God had not cured any leper in Israel and yet she was confident he would cure Naaman. God had ordained this interesting way of spreading knowledge of His greatness.

5:4-6 And one went in, and told his lord, saying, Thus and thus said the maid who is of the land of Israel. And the king of Syria said, Go now, and I will send a letter unto the king of Israel. And he departed, and took with him ten talents of silver, and six thousand pieces of gold, and ten changes of raiment. And he brought the letter to the king of Israel, saying, Now when this letter is come unto thee, behold I have sent with it Naaman, my servant to thee, that thou mayest cure him of his leprosy.

The Syrian king spared no expense in taking immediate action upon hearing of the possibility of his favored military commander being healed. Ten talents of silver would have weighed approximately 750 pounds. Had just the silver been sent, this alone would have been an expensive treasure since no silver was found in the land of Syria.

Possibly in keeping with proper protocol, the Syrian King, Benhadad II, addressed his request directly to Jehoram, son of Ahab, the king of Israel, even though the child-slave had reported that there was a prophet in Israel who could cure his disease. His letter revealed he expected that the king himself would accomplish this healing. This

Syrian king had no knowledge of the true and living God who is merciful and kind to all. He asked that Naaman be healed with no thought of the <u>miracle of conversion</u> Naaman was to receive. He apparently had no understanding of what a prophet of the Lord was or of what God could do through him. Perhaps the words of the child-slave were misquoted to the king. Exactly what happened is not clear.

5:7 And it came to pass, when the king of Israel had read the letter, that he rent (tore) his clothes, and said, Am I God, to kill and to make alive, that this man doth send unto me to cure a man of leprosy? Wherefore consider, I pray you, and see how he seeketh a quarrel against me.

Imagine the dilemma of King Jehoram who felt King Benhadad II had spoken blasphemy knowing that only God could heal disease. He responded by renting (tearing) his clothes as Jews customarily did when blasphemy was encountered.

Note that Barnabus and Paul did this when they were hailed as gods. **(Acts 14:11-15)** The magistrates did likewise when they heard that Paul and Silas were accused of blasphemous deeds. **(Acts 16:22)** And the high priest rent (tore) his clothes, and said of Jesus, "He hath spoken blasphemy." **(Matthew 26:65 and Mark 14:63)**

King Jehoram concluded that he had been given an impossible request in order to provoke him into a war that he was not equipped to win. Neither did he obligate himself by accepting the tremendous bounty offered.

5:8 And it was, when Elisha, the man of God had heard that the king of Israel had rent (tore) his clothes, that he sent to the king, saying, Why hast thou torn thy clothes? Let him come now to me, and he shall know that there is a prophet in Israel.

This is where the sovereign omnipotent God stated His purpose and desire - that Naaman (and actually others too) would know that there was a prophet in Israel and that this prophet knew his God. The wonder is that King Jehoram didn't think of Elisha himself, since he had helped him greatly in the matter of the bloodless war with Moab. **(2nd Kings 3)** Perhaps he was too unnerved by the letter, which he perceived to be blasphemous.

Though disappointed, Naaman did as he was instructed and traveled along with his entourage approximately twenty-five painfully hot miles to the city of Samaria where Elisha resided. Once there, his hopes were further diminished by the additional instructions he received.

5:9-10 So Naaman came with his horses and with his chariot, and stood at the door of the house of Elisha. And Elisha sent a messenger unto him, saying, Go and wash in the Jordan seven times, and thy flesh shall come again to thee, and thou shalt be clean.

5:11-12 But Naaman was angry, and went away, and said, Behold, I thought he will surely come out to me, and stand, and call upon the name of the Lord his God, and strike his hand over the place, and cure the leprosy. Are not Abana and Pharpar, rivers in Damascus, better than all the waters of Israel? May I not wash in them, and be clean? So he turned and went away in a rage.

He said, "Behold, I thought." Thoughts can be the source of our deepest disappointments, resentments, and despair. As a helpless, hopeless man in a pitifully painful condition, we can appreciated that he reacted with understandable rage.

When we presuppose how and when God going to do something, we're setting ourselves up for disillusionment and frustration.

Levitical law taught God's people that uncleanness could be passed from one person to another by touching. Did Naaman think that Elisha had rejected him to avoid touching a leper?

Much to his merit, Naaman's thought that Elisha would "call upon the name of the Lord his God," was absolutely right. What he didn't know was that he, too, would be calling upon and worshiping the Lord God of Israel. How beautiful is our God and how high above are His ways!

Both the river Abana and Pharpar flowed down from mountains and contained clear pure water. These rivers were understandably more suitable to wash in. Our preference is not a factor when it comes to obeying God though.

Mark 1:5 tells of John baptizing repentant sinners in the river Jordan and none were reluctant to do so.

5:13 And his servants came near, and spoke unto him, and said, My father, if the prophet had bid thee to do some great thing, wouldest thou not have done it? How much rather then, when he saith to thee, Wash, and be clean?

It would be wise to hesitate approaching and speaking to a military commander who was in a rage and especially one who had authority over you. It is commendable that Naaman's servants spoke so tenderly to him expressing deep concern for his well-being. Addressing him as, "My father," strongly implies their devotion. Fortunately for everyone, Naaman's servants didn't feed his angry resentment by offering to avenge him. What awful consequences would have occurred if they had! Though disappointed and his hopes crushed, he followed the seemingly unreasonable prescription of the prophet and the counsel of his servants. This man Naaman was unusual, and God saw in him a heart that would yield.

5:14 Then went he down, and dipped himself seven times in the Jordan, according to the saying of the man of God; and his flesh came again like unto the flesh of a little child, and he was clean.

This miracle was wrought in such a way that no man, whether king or prophet, could receive the glory that was due to God alone. We can only imagine the change in this suddenly cleansed and healed man. His life of despair and hopelessness had ended. You know the flesh of a little child is tender and soft not callous or scarred. "Like the flesh of a little child" may remind you of the "little maid" who had been providentially placed in an undesirable circumstance not of her choosing. But God had chosen her to bring knowledge of Him to a well-loved Syrian supreme army commander. The next verse revealed his heartfelt gratitude.

5:15-16 And he returned to the man of God, he and all his company, and came, and stood before him. And he said, Behold, now I know that there is no God in all the earth, but in Israel; now, therefore, I pray thee, take a blessing of thy servant. But he said, As the Lord liveth, before whom I stand, I will receive none. And he urged him to take it, but he refused.

Elisha received the healed man along with his astonished entourage as he returned to give glory to God alone. Naaman said that "now I know there is no God in all the earth, but in Israel." What a life changing revelation! Had he seen lepers commonly healed, he may not have recognized what great compassion the God of Israel had bestowed on him.

You may recall the first hostile opposition to Jesus' ministry occurred when He said to the Jews, "And many lepers were in Israel in the time of Elisha, the prophet, and <u>none</u> of them was cleansed, but only <u>Naaman the Syrian</u>." **(Luke 4:27)**

Naaman offered the king's gifts to the prophet of God who, though he had need, refused to accept them. Elisha's concern for the reputation of the God he served outweighed the desire for earthly rewards. Matthew 6:4 and Luke 6:13 both tell us that we "cannot serve God and mammon (money)."

This matter had been settled in Elisha's heart long before the dazzling gifts arrived. This is what is known as integrity, and it is much needed today. Receiving the gifts could possibly have been construed as "buying a healing."

Verse 5:17 is one of those scriptures we gladly rush through or entirely leap over without understanding its unclear meaning. Here it is:

5:17 And Naaman said, Shall there not then, I pray thee, be given to thy servant two mules' burden of earth? For thy servant will henceforth offer neither burnt offering nor sacrifice unto other gods, but unto the Lord.

The question is: why in the world would anyone want two sacks of dirt? Naaman felt he needed Israelite soil on which to build a mound to worship on when he returned to Damascus believing that a god could only be worshiped on the soil from the nation he governed. Like us, he had a lot to learn about Jehovah God. His humble request evidenced his sincerity.

His being delivered from idolatry was far greater than his being healed of leprosy. Naaman had now pledged before Elisha that he will "henceforth," meaning, "from this point forward" forsake "little g gods" and turn to "the Lord" (Hebrew #3068 meaning, "Jehovah").

5:18 In this thing Lord pardon thy servant, that when my master goeth into the house of Rimmon to worship there, and he leaneth on my hand, and I bow down myself in the house of Rimmon, the Lord pardon thy servant in this thing.

Here is Naaman's only recorded prayer, wherein he asked Jehovah God to overlook that, due to his life's circumstance, he must continue to function as he did before the miracle and his conversion. We, too, may find ourselves in ungodly relationships and/or circumstances that can't be easily changed or gotten out of upon our conversion. Just as God directed this man to Elisha, he can direct him on to an uncompromised life.

Naaman had been changed by the providence of Jehovah God. Surely his entire household, including the unnamed child-slave, was changed upon witnessing the marvelous mercy of God. God had far exceeded the child-slave's desire for him to be healed. We can only imagine her reaction to seeing him healed, cleansed, and converted to the Living God.

Rimmon was a Syrian idol that the Bible only mentions here although this name was also given to a man and to a city mentioned elsewhere.

1st Kings 16:30 tells us that King Ahab did evil in the sight of the Lord above all who were before him. And yet **1st Kings 18:3** states that Obadiah was governor over the house of Ahab and that he feared the Lord greatly. Additional scriptures reveal that, despite these challenging circumstances, Obadiah was able to remain faithful to God. Uncompromised integrity is too important to risk losing. Our God does make a way where there seems to be no way!

5:19-21 And he said unto him, Go in peace. So he departed from him a little way. But Gehazi, the servant of Elisha, the man of God, said, Behold, my master hath spared Naaman, this Syrian, in not receiving at his hands that which he brought: but, as the Lord liveth, I will run after him, and take somewhat of him. So Gehazi followed after Naaman. And when Naaman saw him running after him, he alighted from the chariot to meet him, and said, Is all well?

Gehazi is described as "the servant of Elisha," when perhaps he could have been described as "the self-serving servant" instead. Darkness is as the noonday to God. He doesn't need a light bulb to see a man's heart. Here He chose to reveal the inner thoughts of Gehazi just as He will our thoughts on judgment day. **(1st Corinthians 4:5)** Notice that Naaman had only gone "a little way" before Gehazi conceived a wicked deed in his heart.

Mark 7:21 lists the thirteen evil things that proceed from the heart of men and produce defilement. Is it surprising that the first of these is "evil thoughts?"

The expression, "as the Lord liveth," was a way for Gehazi to express his firm resolve and definitely was not a pledge to God to do this ungodly deed. Elisha had used the same phrase when declaring his firm resolve not to receive a reward.

Naaman recognized him as the prophet's servant, and, because he was running as fast as his feet could carry him, Naaman wondered what the cause was. Greed was the cause, my friend.

Proverbs 15:27 states plainly, "He that is greedy for gain troubleth his own house."

And we will see shortly how greatly Gehazi troubled his own house for generations to come!

5:22-23 And he said, All is well. My master hath sent me, saying, Behold, even now there are come to me from Mount Ephraim two young men of the sons of the prophets: give them, I pray thee, a talent of silver, and two changes of garments. And Naaman said, Be content, take two talents. And he urged him, and bound two talents of silver in two bags, with two changes of garments, and laid them upon two of his servants, and they bore them before him.

This is where the plot was hatched and began to grow. Not only did Gehazi say his master had sent him, he furthermore concocted the false story of the sons of the prophets. He asked for a silver talent and two changes of garments. Naaman generously gave him two talents of silver, plus the garments. This wouldn't be the last time Gehazi got more than he asked for.

5:24 And when he came to the tower, he took them from their hand, and bestowed them in the house; and he let the men go, and they departed.

Gehazi stashed the stuff out of sight. If the men perceived the wickedness in him, I imagine they were glad to depart from him and the seventy-five pounds of silver each carried.

5:25 But he went in, and stood before his master. And Elisha said unto him, From where comest thou, Gehazi? And he said, thy servant went not here or there.

The last words he spoke before judgment was pronounced upon him and on his descendants were all lies. Up to this point, he had felt completely justified.

Truly, as it is written in Jeremiah **17:9-10**, "The heart is deceitful above all things, and desperately wicked, who can know it? I, the Lord, search the heart, I test the conscience, even to give every man according to his ways, and according to the fruit of his doings."

5:26-27 And he said unto him, Went not mine heart with thee, when the man turned from his chariot to meet thee? Is it a time to receive money, and to receive garments, and olive yards, and vineyards, and sheep, and oxen, and menservants, and maidservants? The leprosy, therefore, of Naaman shall cleave (cling) unto thee, and unto thy seed forever. And he went out from his presence a leper as white as snow.

Gehazi never answered Elisha's two questions. He had said earlier in his heart that he desired to "take something from" Naaman. He certainly did take something, my friend! And it was something he didn't want and couldn't get rid of. "As white as snow" reveals that his leprosy was in full bloom and not in blotches as in an early stage. It's a wonder that this man was so close to Elisha and yet his heart was far away.

Gehazi's deceitfully acquired 150 pounds of silver could not have purchased health or right standing with God. His heart was not pure just as Judas Iscariot's heart wasn't even though he was with Jesus a long time.

Gehazi's greed could have alienated Naaman from the God of Israel. Elisha had showed him there was a difference between Jehovah God and the "little g gods." There's no record of an attempt by Elisha to correct any possible wrong conclusion drawn by Naaman through the evil deed of Gehazi. But God is His own defender and is well able to right the wrong done.

OH, GOD, REMEMBER ME!

King David wrote:
Psalm 139:16 Thine eyes did see my substance, yet being unformed; and in thy book all my <u>members</u> (Hebrew #3338 meaning, "parts") were written ...

By this scripture we know that He has seen and known us individually. He has prescribed all the <u>members</u> or parts of our being.

We live in a time when lives are being "dis-membered." Lives are being torn apart by divorce, indebtedness, and by loved-ones who have strayed from the love of the truth. God wants you to know that for those whom He has "membered," He can also "re-member." He desires to heal your life's deepest agonies, disappointments, and failures.

However, there are some things He chooses not to "re-member." The writer of Hebrews quoted **Jeremiah 31:34** verbatim when, in Chapter 8:12, he wrote:
"For I will be merciful unto their unrighteousness, and their sins and their iniquities will I <u>remember</u> no more."

The writer of Hebrews also quoted from **Jeremiah 31:33** in Chapter 10:16-17 where we are assured by these words:
"This is the covenant I will make with them after those days, saith the Lord: I will put my laws into their hearts,

and in their minds will I write them, and their sins and iniquities will I <u>remember</u> no more."

In these verses, God twice used the phrase, "will I remember no more" as He stated what He willfully chooses to do.

God's word teaches that whenever He <u>remembers</u> someone, He also moves on their behalf. That's worth repeating. When God <u>remembers</u> someone, He also moves on their behalf.

In this study, we will learn of eleven occasions where God moved when He remembered.

The last person the Bible speaks of who asked to be remembered was the thief on the cross. And, you know what Jesus promised him. The first person to be remembered by God was Noah. After the flood waters prevailed upon the earth a 150 days, we are told:

Genesis 8:1 And God <u>remembered</u> Noah, and every living thing, and all the cattle that was with him in the ark: and God made a wind to pass over the earth, and the waters subsided.

When God <u>remembered</u> Noah, He moved on his behalf. Further on in Genesis, we are told what God did when He <u>remembered</u> Abraham.

Genesis 19:29 And it came to pass, when God destroyed the cities of the plain, that God <u>remembered</u>

Abraham, and sent Lot out of the midst of the overthrow …

Do you know someone who needs to be remembered by God and delivered from the midst of the overthrow?

Genesis 30:22 God <u>remembered</u> Rachel, and God harkened unto her, and opened her womb.

Moses wrote these words of the Hebrews living in Egyptian bondage:
    Exodus 2:24 And God heard their groaning, and God <u>remembered</u> his covenant with Abraham, with Isaac, and with Jacob.

God then moved on their behalf by sending an angel to direct Moses to become their deliverer. He stated to Moses His awareness of their helplessness and pledged to <u>move</u> on their behalf.

    Exodus 6:5 And I have also heard the groaning of the children of Israel, whom the Egyptians have kept in bondage; and I have <u>remembered</u> my covenant.

God then spoke six "I will" declarations of what He planned to <u>move</u> and do on their behalf. When God remembers, He moves.

    1st Samuel begins with the heart-rending story of Hannah being relentlessly provoked by her adversary <u>because God</u> had chosen to shut her womb. This continued until Hannah ultimately prayed the prayer God was waiting to answer. Scripture says that she was in "bitterness of soul," and that she "wept bitterly," as she prayed:

   1st Samuel 1:11 O Lord of hosts, if you will indeed look on the affliction of your handmaid, and <u>remember me</u> ...

As you know, she was <u>remembered</u> and bore a son. She named him Samuel saying, "Because I have asked him of the Lord."

God did exceedingly abundantly above all that she asked or thought. **(Ephesians 3:20)** In **Chapter 2 of 1st Samuel** we learn that she later bore three sons and two daughters. All of this happened **after** she prayed to be remembered. When God remembers, He moves.

Nehemiah served God during a time of great distress when the Jewish exiles were permitted to return to their homeland from captivity in Babylon. His God-given assignment was to rebuild the protecting wall surrounding Jerusalem. It was indeed a daunting task. Is it any wonder that the thirteen chapters in the book of Nehemiah record him praying eleven times? Carrying such a crushing burden, the final chapter records him praying three times, "Remember me, O my God."
(Nehemiah 13:14, 13:22, 13:31)

When Jeremiah was cursed by his own people, he pleaded, "O Lord, thou knowest; <u>remember me</u>, and visit me. His plea recorded in **Jeremiah 15:15** moved God to respond with five "I will" declarations of what He promised to do.

Hezekiah was at the point of death and in great anguish of soul when he cried out to God to be remembered.

2nd Kings 20:3 I beseech thee, O Lord, remember, now how I have walked before thee in truth and with a perfect heart, and have done that which is good in thy sight. And Hezekiah wept sore (very much).

God hearkened to his request to be remembered and extended his life fifteen years.

When God reveals failure in the character of one of His children, He doesn't do it so others with similar faults can ridicule or scorn. Character flaws are revealed so He can demonstrate His mercy and redeeming love.

Let's consider a man whose life was an absolute failure. This man was a reprobate, was morally depraved and lived his entire life in rebellion against God and His calling upon his life. He died disgraced and humiliated at the hands of the enemies of God. I have heard his life preached, and I have read it for myself. The tale of his life is disgusting to me.

I asked God to let me understand why He has given this man a place of honor by listing his name in the eleventh chapter of Hebrews known as the "Faith Hall of Fame." Why would God choose to honor him as he did others whose faith had pleased him? People like Abraham, Isaac, Jacob, Joseph, Samuel, and King David? Why would God choose to honor this man whose heart was corrupt?

Like Jesus, his impending conception was announced by an angel who named him before his birth. He was born to Godly parents who earnestly sought God on how to raise him up. **(Judges 13:12)**

Judges 13:5 tells us that he was to be a Nazarite from his mother's womb. It also tells us that God desired to use him to begin to deliver His people out of the hands of their enemies the Philistines. He lived during a time, because of Israel's rebellion, God had turned them over to their enemies.

From the time of his birth, scripture says that God blessed him. And, as he grew, the Spirit of God would move upon him at times. God's purpose was for him to live separate unto Him. But he didn't care about God or the things pertaining to holiness. He had no regard whatsoever for the calling and purposes of God. He lived his entire life engulfed in sinful pleasure. He was truly a heartbreaker. He disappointed his parents' expectations. He broke their heart. And he grieved the heart of God.

A Nazarite was not to touch any dead person or animal. He was not to eat anything that came from the vine. He was to be separate from all appearance of evil. He broke every one of the Nazarite vows.

At the close of Samson's lust-driven life, with his eyes having been gouged out at the hands of his enemies, he was forced to ground meal as a beast would do.

He was called out to entertain his captors while about three thousand men and women cheered on a rooftop, making sport of him. As he stood between two middle pillars on which the house stood, he prayed, "O Lord God, <u>remember me</u>, I pray thee, and strengthen me ..."
(Judges 16:28)

At the moment of Samson's death, God empowered him to fulfill his calling and purpose to <u>begin to deliver</u> His people. He destroyed the house of the Philistine god and brought sudden death to the thousands of Philistines who had gathered to mock him.

What do you suppose is one of the greatest fears in the heart of someone who truly loves God? King David expressed his greatest fear in **Psalm 51**, which he wrote after the prophet Nathan exposed his greatest sins of adultery and murder.

    Psalm 51:11 Cast me not away from thy presence and take not thy Holy Spirit from me.

King David never pleaded, "O, God, take not my kingdom, my possessions, my power from me." His greatest concern was for the loss of the presence of God. Secular psychologists recognize that a basic fear in children is that of being abandoned. Jesus understood this and was careful to reassure His followers that He would not abandon them. His very last words recorded in Matthew are:

Matthew 28: ... Lo, I am with you always, even to the end of the world.

It's sad that Samson was so self-consumed that according to **Judges 16:20** he knew not that the Lord had departed from him.

What a contrast that is to Job. Samson suffered the consequences of his own sin, but God said that Job was perfect and upright and that "he sinned not, nor charged God foolishly." **(Job 1:22)** Job never prayed to have his health restored. He never prayed to have his children, his friends, or his wealth restored. His only concern was for the loss of the presence of God. He was overwhelmed by an intense desire to know why God had departed from him. He even cried, "For the thing which I greatly feared is come upon me, and that which I was afraid of is come unto me." **(Job 3:25)** He was frantically searching to find the presence of God again and to understand why he had been forsaken. What a contrast to Samson who did not even notice that the Spirit of God had departed.

Job 19:23 (Job speaking) Oh, that my words were now written! Oh, that they were printed in a book ...

He continued in **23:3** where he pleaded to see God. He didn't ask to see his children again. His desire was only to see God.

Job 23:3 Oh, that I knew where I might find him, and that I might come even unto his seat! I would set my cause before him, and fill my mouth with arguments. I would know the words which he would answer me, and <u>understand</u> what he would say to me. Behold I go forward, but he is not there; and backward, but I cannot perceive him. But he knoweth the way that I take; when he hath tested me, I shall come forth as gold. But he is of one mind, and who can turn him? And what his soul desireth, even that he doeth. For he performeth the thing that is appointed for me; and many such things are with him.

In **Job 14:14**, he cried:
All the days of my appointed time will I wait, till my change come. Thou shalt call, and I will answer thee; thou will have a desire to the work of thine hands. Oh, that thou wouldest appoint me a set time, and <u>remember me</u>!

With his life having been dis-membered by Satan, the cry of his heart was to be re-membered by God. We are told at the close:

Job 42:12 So the Lord blessed the latter end of Job more than his beginning ...

Many lives today have been dis-membered. Many need to be re-membered by God and for Him to move and accomplish His will and purpose.

Being remembered by God puts you in company with: Noah, Abraham, Rachel, Hannah, King Hezekiah, Jeremiah, Nehemiah, the Hebrew children, Samson, Job, and the thief on the cross. None of these were disappointed by the response from God. As He remembered them, He moved on their behalf.

Do you need for God to re-member you and put all the members of your life together in a way that only He can? He is waiting this very moment for you to ask.

Here is a marvelous promise from the word of God: **Malachi 3:16-17** Then they that feared the Lord spoke often one to another; and the Lord harkened, and heard it, and a book of remembrance was written before him for them that feared the Lord, and that thought upon his name. And they shall be mine, saith the Lord of hosts, in that day when I make up my jewels; and I will spare them, as a man spareth his own son that serveth him.

POUR OUT YOUR HEART

(Scriptures are from 1st Kings unless otherwise noted)

Scriptures describe people and events in such a way as to let the reader "get the picture" so to speak.

1st Kings 16:29-32 tells us that King Ahab reigned over Israel in Samaria twenty-two years and that he did evil above all who were before him. Verse 32 continues by saying, "... as if it had been a light thing for him to walk in the sins of Jeroboam ... he took as his wife Jezebel and went and served Baal and worshiped him."

Jezebel was the daughter of a Sidonian king. Wives from these heathen people also caused Solomon to sin grossly even to the extent of offering his children as live sacrifices. **(Nehemiah 13:26)**

The conclusion of this chapter states that Ahab did more to provoke the Lord God of Israel to anger than all the kings of Israel before him. **(1st Kings 16:33)**

The first mention of Elijah is in **1st Kings 17:1** where he is introduced as "Elijah, the Tishbite." He is the only person in scripture referred to as "a Tishbite." Five later scriptures refer to him as 'the Tishbite' and three others as "Elijah, the prophet."

His boldness is appreciated more when we consider that he does not, at this beginning of the recorded portion of his ministry, have a reputation of being a prophet of God. The name Elijah is a Hebrew word (#4520) meaning, "Whose God is Jehovah." Through the ordained events of this man's life, Jehovah God will become known.

The wickedness of Ahab was stressed to emphasize the boldness of the little known Elijah as he waltzed into the presence of the most evil king who had ever lived and announced who he represented and not who he was.

Ahab is the king of Israel, but he does not know the KING OF ISRAEL, THE KING OF KINGS, and THE LORD OF LORDS. Notice that Elijah doesn't address him as king; only as Ahab. In fact, scripture records no one addressing him as King Ahab. He is only called "Ahab king of Israel."

1st Kings 17:1 ... Ahab, as the Lord God of Israel liveth, <u>before whom I stand</u>, there shall not be dew nor rain these years, but according to my word.

The phrase "before whom I stand" is used only four times in scripture; three times by Elijah and once by Elisha. Elijah was letting Ahab know who His God was and that he was accountable to Him alone. Not only would there be no rain, but also no dew. It seems as though God had had enough!

Nowhere in scripture are we told that Elijah foretold of a three-year drought. He himself did not know how long this drought would last. It could have lasted two months or perhaps 200 years. God works by His determinate counsel and moves at His appointed time.

Ahab did not ask the reason for this judgment and neither did he question it. The fact that Ahab believed what Elijah said is proved by his not having him killed on the spot.

Thirteen famines are recorded in Israel's history. The drought pronounced by Elijah resulted in a severe famine as God brought judgment against a rebellious people. Just as we are only given further instruction after obeying God, Elijah was then told to "get thee from hence" and go to the Brook Cherith. **(1st Kings 17:3)** He was to "hide himself" and receive provision from God made available by the brook and by ravens. This mighty man of God would experience the drought of unknown length and its resulting famine just as all Israel would, but God assured him that his needs would be met.

1st Kings 17:7 And it came to pass after awhile, that the brook dried up, because there had been no rain in the land.

Yes, we are affected by conditions imposed as judgment upon others, but our provision comes from God.

Speaking of those who are upright before the Lord:
Psalm 37:19 They shall not be ashamed in the evil time; and in the days of famine they shall be satisfied.

God directed Elijah to the unnamed widow whom He had commanded to sustain him. He obeyed and God provided. This was the second time God had told him where to go and how He would provide. Elijah assured the widow that God would continue to provide until He sent rain upon the earth. Apparently, he was there for quite some time, because **1st Kings 17:18** begins by saying the drought was now in its third year.

Have you ever thought that during the three year time span Elijah must have wondered when God would permit the drought to end? Remember he had told Ahab there would be no dew or rain other than by his word. As a servant delivering a message, he didn't know what he would have to endure.

The God who told Elijah to "hide himself" then told him to "go show thyself unto Ahab, and I will send rain upon the earth." **(1st Kings 18:1)** You go and I will do.

Some emphasize Ahab and Jezebel as the objects of this dramatic story. However, the true drama concerned "all of the people" who would be called on to make a choice. Ahab and Jezebel were not called on to make a choice. They had already made their choices. The phrase "all the people" was used five times in **Chapter 18**. Truly, "all the people" are the actual focus of this intense episode. God called upon "all the people" to relinquish, renounce, and release their idolatrous worship, as we will see as the story unfolds.

1st Kings 18 reveals the providential moving of the Lord. Then, in the third year of drought, God told Elijah to "<u>GO</u> show himself to Ahab." At the same time Ahab told Obadiah to <u>GO</u> look for grass for their animals which was very scarce after three years without moisture.

1st Kings 18:3 states that Obadiah was governor of Ahab's house and that he feared the Lord greatly. Ahab was more evil than the six wicked kings who had reigned before him. Here we find this God-fearing man, Obadiah, serving as governor of his house. That was a challenging position.

The next time you feel you are required to serve God under difficult or impossible circumstances consider this man, Obadiah. These passages reveal that he was able to save a hundred of the Lord's prophets whom Jezebel desired to murder. His life's circumstance was unpleasant and undesirable, and yet he had been placed there as part of God's providential plan to save others. Maybe we shouldn't fret so much over being placed in less than desirable circumstances. After all, God might use us to save a hundred just as He used this faithful man Obadiah.

Verse 17 begins with the sharp greeting of Ahab as he met Elijah and is followed by Elijah's direct rebuttal in verse 18.

1st Kings 18:17-18 And it came to pass, when Ahab saw Elijah, that Ahab said unto him, 'Art thou he who troubleth Israel?" And he answered, I have not troubled Israel; but thou, and thy father's house, in that ye have forsaken the commandments of the Lord, and thou hast followed Baalim.

I like Elijah. He was straightforward, didn't mince words, and didn't waste time trying to persuade those who would not be persuaded. As mentioned earlier, this drama is not so much about the wickedness of Ahab and Jezebel as it is about "all the people." These are the ones God had sent Elijah to persuade. In case you are wondering, "Baalim" is the plural of "Baal," the "little g god" shamefully worshiped by Israel and Judea at that time.

Remarkably, Ahab did all Elijah told him to do. He gathered ALL of Israel, plus four hundred fifty prophets of Baal, and four hundred other false prophets who ate at Jezebel's table. **(1st Kings 18:19)** Mount Carmel must have been pretty crowded that day.

Elijah addressed his question to "all the people" and not to Ahab, Jezebel, or the prophets.

1st Kings 18:21 And Elijah came unto <u>all the people</u>, and said, "How long halt ye between two opinions? If the Lord be God, then follow him; but if Baal, then follow him. And the people answered him not a word.

These people were supposed to have knowledge of God and to reverence and serve Him. They answered not a word, because they knew they were wrong. He then set up a demonstration to determine which God was God. There's nothing like a visible manifestation of the power of God during a crisis to gain our full focus. What we feel is a difficult time is really "promotion time" for those who choose to walk with the Lord.

In verse 22, Elijah again addressed "<u>all the people</u>." Verse 24 records that <u>all the people</u> agreed that the God who answered by fire was God.

You may be familiar with what happened when the false prophets offered their sacrifice and began to call upon their "little g god." Their false god did not answer just like "<u>all the people</u>" did not answer when Elijah questioned them.

What a racket that must have been with eight hundred fifty prophets crying from morning until noon and asking their god to hear them. Elijah began to mock and ridicule their god, and their efforts to get him to respond. **(1st Kings 18:27)** They cried aloud and cut themselves to no avail. When the midday passed, they continued prophesying until time of the evening sacrifice. There was neither any voice from their god, nor any answer.

What a contrast to our God who answers while we are yet speaking. **(Isaiah 65:24)**

In verse 30 Elijah again spoke to "<u>all the people</u>" and said, "Come near unto me." This is being emphasized so you will appreciate that this drama was about "<u>all the people</u>" and the choice they were called upon to make. Elijah does not call to Ahab, Jezebel, or the false prophets to "Come near unto me."

Elijah repaired the altar, which had been torn apart by the rampage of the frustrated false prophets. He used twelve stones in honor of the twelve tribes of Israel. He then made a trench to surround the altar. After placing the sacrifice on the altar, he made an outrageous request in verse 33 "... fill four barrels with <u>water</u>, and <u>pour</u> it on the burnt sacrifice (sacrifice to be burned), and on the wood." And he added to their quandary by requiring even greater sacrifice in verse 34, "And he said do it a second time. And they did it a second time. And he said do it a third time. And they did it a third time."

The man of God required three pourings totaling twelve barrels of what they needed to sustain life. Water was their most precious possession. Their lives and the lives of their children depended on what was stored in the barrels, or so they thought. Do you think maybe anyone there was wondering something like: "Man of God, where in the world have you been the last three years while there has been no rain and no dew? Who do you think you are to ask us to do such a thing as this?" Curiously, they obeyed without knowing if he would require them to pour out 300 or 3,000 barrels.

The fact that they complied was as astounding as the request itself. Talk about a sacrifice! Not one barrel, not one pouring; but four barrels poured three times. We read that the famine, which was caused by the drought, was severe. Wasn't it enough that two bullocks were required for the sacrifice? That's asking a great deal from people living in a severe famine. And then to be required to <u>pour out</u> the most precious thing they had!

Elijah's three requests were absurd. Was anyone thinking, "How about sacrificing sand or rocks? We have an abundance of sand and rocks, and we'll never miss them. But, water? That's asking way too much!" Mankind may be willing to give generously when what he gives costs him nothing.

Verses 36-37 reveal this prophet's heart toward God. We've noted how confident Elijah was when he addressed Ahab. How scornful Elijah was when he mocked the false prophets, and how directly Elijah spoke unto "<u>all the people</u>." When calling upon Jehovah God, Elijah is not haughty or scornful: he appealed to God as His servant.

1st Kings 18:36-37 And it came to pass at the time of the offering of the evening sacrifice, that <u>Elijah, the prophet</u>, came near, and said, "LORD God of Abraham, Isaac, and of Israel, let it be known this day that thou art God in Israel, and that I am thy servant, and that I have done all these things at thy word. Hear me, O LORD, hear me, that this people may know that thou art the LORD God, and that thou hast turned their heart back again.

This scripture, like two others, refers to him as, "<u>Elijah, the prophet</u>." He approached God by acknowledging that He was the God of their forefathers: Abraham, Isaac, and Israel (Jacob). Certainly "<u>all the people</u>" knew that a "little g god" was not the God of their forefathers. Elijah simply prayed, "I am your servant." Whether you are a prince or a pauper, the only goal you should strive for is to be His servant. Elijah's earnest desire was that God would make Himself known unto "<u>all the people</u>" and that their hearts would be turned back to the Lord.

1st Kings 18:38-39 Then the fire of the Lord fell, and consumed the burnt sacrifice, and the wood, and the stones, and the dust, and licked up the water that was in the trench. And when <u>all of the people</u> saw it, they fell on their faces: and they said, The LORD, he is God; the LORD, he is God.

All throughout this drama "<u>all the people</u>" are the ones God intended to win back to Him in this "contest." Like <u>all the people</u>, can you say, "<u>The Lord, He is God; the Lord, He is God!!</u>"

God caused this lesson to be compiled in order to give understanding of the age-old story of Elijah's showdown with Ahab, the false prophets, and the backslidden people of God. But that's not all God intended.

Remember reading earlier that the people would be called upon to <u>relinquish, renounce, and release</u>? The Spirit of the Living God is here to ask you to do the same.

Have you been burdened and hindered by holding onto the precious things stored in your barrels? Barrels can hold great quantities of hurts and disappointments. Barrels can store corrosive bitterness and self-pity.

No one can run this race, much less win it, while dragging barrels loaded with regret. Pour out your barrels as a sacrifice to God. Pour out your plans for your own fulfilment. Relinquish stubbornness. Renounce your "God, you have to move this way" approach.

Psalm 62:8 (Written by King David) Trust in him at all times, ye people; <u>pour out your heart</u> before him.

You do not need a contingency action plan. Let go and let God! Release them now. Your barrels of precious things held in reserve may be limiting the Holy One of Israel.

Speaking of Messiah's suffering and death:

Isaiah 53:12 ... <u>He hath poured out his soul unto death</u>.

And now, the call has gone forth for you to <u>pour out your soul unto Him</u>.

Matthew 7:13 Enter by the narrow gate; for wide is the gate and broad is the way that leads to destruction, and there are many who go in by it.

Luke 13:24 Strive to enter through the narrow gate, for many, I say to you, will seek to enter and will not be able.

How in the world are you going to enter in through the narrow gate dragging all that you've treasured up in your barrels? When all you have left is a pile of ashes, you'll know God has received your sacrifice. As your desire for Him increases, He has promised to give you beauty for those ashes. **(Isaiah 61:3)**

PROVOKED TO PRAYER

(All verses from 1st Samuel unless otherwise listed)

1st Samuel 1:1 Now there was a certain man of Ramathaimzophim, of Mount Ephraim, and his name was Elkanah, the son of Tohu, the son of Zuph, an Ephraimite.

The exact location of Ramathaimzophim is not known, but it is believed to have been four or five miles northwest of Jerusalem where present-day Neby Samwil (meaning, "the prophet Samuel") is located. It's the place of Samuel's birth and the place of his death. It may be the Arimathea of the New Testament.

1:2 And he had two wives: the name of the one was Hannah, and the name of the other, Peninnah. And Peninnah had children, but Hannah had no children.

Hannah is mentioned only in 1st Samuel chapters one and two where her name appears eleven times. Hannah, a Hebrew name (#2584), means "favor and grace." We will learn that God bestowed abundant favor and grace upon her in the most difficult of circumstances.

God ordained monogamy from the beginning. Polygamy, though not expressly forbidden in the Old Testament, falls short of God's ideal for marriage. Old Testament accounts significantly reveal the misery and unhappiness resulting from polygamous families.

Verse 2 immediately identified the problem. And in just a few more verses we'll learn how God worked to bring about the victory He had desired before allowing the problem to exist. Glory to His name! He may choose to do that in your life too.

In order to accomplish His desire, He allowed Hannah to be in this undesirable circumstance. And it was a circumstance that she did not choose and one that she could not change. Have you experienced something similar?

1:3 And this man went up out of his city yearly to worship and to sacrifice unto the Lord of hosts in Shiloh. And the two sons of Eli, Hophni and Phinehas, the priests of the Lord, were there.

Hophni and Phinehas were called priests here because Eli was very old and had assigned the active duties of his office to his sons. Although they were called priests, we learn later in Chapter 2:12 that their character was as "sons of Belial" or the devil.

1:4-5 And when the time was that Elkanah offered, he gave to Peninnah, his wife, and to all her sons and her daughters, portions. But unto Hannah, he gave a worthy portion; for he loved Hannah: but the Lord had shut her womb.

It's apparent that Elkanah had ample means to meet the needs of his family and that he loved Hannah and was especially generous to her. But God had ordained something that caused Hannah great anguish. He had shut her womb! She bore the reproach of childlessness without understanding why.

God is sovereign and He works in mysterious ways. He doesn't reveal all of his determinate (definite or fixed) counsel. We are to trust Him and recognize that He is worthy; He is indeed trustworthy.

1:6-7 And her adversary also provoked her sore (relentlessly), to make her fret, because the Lord had shut her womb. And as he did so year by year, when she went up to the house of the Lord, so she provoked her; therefore she wept, and did not eat.

We, too, have an adversary who, according to **1st Peter 5:8**, is "like a roaring lion walketh about, seeking whom he may devour."

It's interesting that the adversary was allowed to provoke her relentlessly and to cause her to fret over a circumstance God had chosen in order to bring about His best for her life and His best for Israel. As a man, Samuel functioned in some ways as a priest; he anointed Israel first two kings; Saul, and David; though he actually was Israel's first prophet.

The adversary who provoked her year by year is referred to in the masculine "he." In the same sentence, we're told that "she provoked her." Obviously, the devil uses people as instruments of provoking (grieving) others. "Year by year" indicates an ongoing never-ending ordeal. Her weeping and being unable to eat is evidence of her deep anguish. Hannah was, indeed, grievously vexed.

1:8 Then said Elkanah, her husband, to her, Hannah, why weepest thou? And why eatest thou not? And why is thy heart grieved? Am not I better to thee than ten sons?

Elkanah asked his wife four questions in an attempt to turn her from being grieved to being grateful. She received his wise counsel and was then able to continue. We are told that he loved her and that he knew her. His concern showed that he knew her in an intimate way and that he understood her heart, too.

1st Samuel 1:9-10 So Hannah rose up after they had eaten in Shiloh, and after they had drunk. Now Eli, the priest, sat upon a seat by a post of the temple of the Lord. And she was in bitterness of soul, and prayed unto the Lord, and wept bitterly.

The Book of Ruth records Naomi saying in Chapter 1:20, "... for the Almighty hath dealt very bitterly with me," although leaving her homeland and journeying to Moab had been her choice. In contrast, Hannah did not direct bitter, angry words toward the Lord as Naomi had. Hannah did not blame God for her dilemma, although the scripture tells us that it was the Blessed Controller who had shut her womb.

1:11 And she vowed a vow, and said, 'O LORD of hosts, if thou wilt indeed look upon the affliction of thine handmaid, and remember me, and not forget thine handmaid, but wilt give unto thine handmaid a male (man) child, then I will give him unto the Lord all the days of his life, and there shall be no razor come upon his head.

Hannah made this vow whole-heartedly knowing that God considers our vows before Him as sacred and binding. This is the first time the Bible mentions anyone addressing a prayer to, "O, Lord of hosts."

Psalm 24:10 (Written by King David) The Lord of hosts, he is the King of glory.

The title, "Lord of hosts," is used in time of great need. It recognizes Jehovah as being the Lord of the multitude of warrior hosts. It is not used anywhere in the Pentateuch, or directly in Joshua or Judges, and only occurs rarely in Psalms. The prophet Jeremiah used this term seventy-one times. As Lord of host, God is able to marshal all the hosts of heaven to fulfill His purposes and to help His people.

Hannah was well aware that she was making this solemn vow to the "Lord of hosts." Notice that she said, "If thou wilt look on the affliction of thine handmaid, and remember me." Her heart was humbled before the Lord as she reminded Him that she was His handmaid. Through suffering, her will had become conformed to His; now victory can come forth!

Hannah is not alone in asking God to remember her. Others like Nehemiah, Hezekiah, Jeremiah, Samson, Job, and the thief on the cross all prayed asking God to remember them, and He did! When He remembers someone, He moves to bring forth His counsel and purposes and in a glorious way.

1:12-13 And it came to pass, as she continued praying before the Lord, that Eli marked (observed) her mouth. Now Hannah, she spoke in her heart; only her lips moved, but her voice was not heard. Therefore, Eli thought she was drunk.

Eli observed her mouth and misjudged the intent of her heart. Truly, as **1st Samuel 16:7** says, "… for the Lord seeth not as man seeth; for man looketh on the outward appearance, but the Lord looketh on the heart."

The phrase "it came to pass" is used four times in the first four chapters of 1st Samuel and 452 times throughout the entire Bible. Of course, when we are going through the "going-througher," we feel as though "it came to stay."

James 5:16 The effectual fervent prayer of a righteous man availeth much.

Fervent is a Greek word (#2204) meaning, "to be hot, to boil." If you are not deeply affected by your prayer, don't expect the Lord to be either.

Hannah prayed fervently from her heart, and God was deeply affected, too. Her prayer affected Him so much that He moved on her behalf.

Hebrews 4:15 teaches that Jesus is touched with the feeling of our infirmities and goes on in verse 16 to say, "Let us, therefore, come boldly unto the throne of grace, that we may obtain mercy, and find grace to help in time of need." Oh, how we praise God for the new and living way that is consecrated for us through His Blood!

1:14-18 Now Eli said unto her, How long wilt thou be intoxicated (drunken)? Put away thy wine from thee. And Hannah answered and said, 'No, my lord, I am a woman of a sorrowful spirit. I have drunk neither wine nor strong drink, but have poured out my soul before the Lord. Count not thy handmaid as a wicked woman (a daughter of Belial); for out of the abundance of my complaint and grief have I been speaking. Then Eli answered and said, Go in peace, and the God of Israel grant thee thy petition that thou hast asked of Him. And she said, Let thine handmaid find grace in thy sight. So the woman went her way, and did eat, and her countenance was no more sad.

Hannah addressed Eli as little "l" "lord." The Hebrew word lord (#113) means "ruler, controller, master." She spoke to God as capitol L "Lord" (Hebrew #3068) meaning, "self-existent Eternal God Jehovah." Hannah knew who she was speaking to and also who she was praying to.

Erroneous assumptions based only on what our eyes see can easily be made. Eli judged her on what he thought he saw without seeing his own sons were drunk and engaged with temple prostitutes. He didn't accuse them but he accused her. Interesting. When Eli said she had been "drinking," she told him that she was not drunk, but that she had "poured out" her soul unto God.

He told her to go in peace that her petition would be granted, and, yet, he didn't know her petition or that the answer to her prayer would introduce the prophetic order God had desired. Hannah believed his word, and her actions proved it.

1:19 And they rose up in the morning early, and worshiped before the Lord, and returned, and came to their house at Ramah; and Elkanah knew Hannah, his wife, and the Lord remembered her.

Just as God remembered Rachel in Genesis 30:22, He remembered Hannah and opened her womb.

1:20 Wherefore it came to pass, when the time was come about after Hannah had conceived, that she bore a son, and called his name Samuel, saying, Because I have asked him of the Lord.

Hannah's son was born, and she named him "Samuel," a Hebrew (#8050) name meaning, "heard of God." Hannah knew that she had heard from God and been touched by His marvelous grace.

1:21-23 And the man, Elkanah, and all his house, went up to offer unto the Lord yearly sacrifice, and his vow. But Hannah went not up; for she said unto her husband, I will not go up until the child is weaned, and then I will bring him, that he may appear before the Lord, and there abide forever. And Elkanah, her husband, said unto her, Do what seemeth to thee good; tarry until thou hast weaned him; only the Lord establish his word. So the woman abode and nursed her son until she weaned him.

Scripture does not say that Elkanah was concerned about having this child or even about his upbringing. His only concern was for Hannah's happiness. Hannah's desire was not to out-do or out-produce Peninnah, who had at least four sons and daughters. Hannah knew that, as she fulfilled her promise to God, Samuel would abide forever with Him.

Did you know that agonizing in prayer can purify our motives? It can help remove the dross (or impurities) from our desires. As your yielded heart melts before Him in total surrender and humility, He is able to instill His desire in you. When we pray the prayers He desires, victory is on the way!

1:24 And when she had weaned him, she took him up with her, with three bullocks, and one ephah of flour, and a skin of wine, and brought him unto the house of the Lord in Shiloh; and the child was young.

Some have estimated that Samuel was three years old before being weaned and brought to the house of the Lord. When Hannah brought him, she did not come empty handed. Not only did she bring her only child, as she had promised, but also three young bulls, one ephah of flour which was the unit for dry measure equaling about thirteen quarts, and a skin of wine. Every step of the way, her actions indicated godly sincerity. God is going to reward her far beyond her greatest expectation. But isn't that just like our Father God?

1:25-28 And they slew a bullock, and brought the child to Eli. And she said, 'O my lord, as thy soul liveth, my lord, I am the woman who stood by thee here, praying unto the Lord. For this child I prayed; and the Lord hath given me my petition, which I asked of him. Therefore also I have lent him to the Lord; as long as he liveth he shall be lent to the Lord. And he worshiped the Lord there.

Until now Eli had not known that the cry of her heart had been for a man-child. And he was yet to learn that this child who was "lent to the Lord" would be priest after him and not his own sons as he had intended. Later, Samuel would become Israel's first prophet.

Notice that the verse says, "he worshiped the Lord there." Apparently this is referring to the young child.

The following are the names of seven people mentioned in chapter one: Elkanah, Hannah, Peninnah, Eli, Hophni, Phinehas, and Samuel. None knew God was working to bring about His best for Israel at that time. And He's working to bring about His best in your life too without your awareness or interference. Amazing.

Hannah earned her P.H.D. by making her request known, not unto the priest, but unto the Lord of hosts. Hannah's P.H.D. was earned through earnest prayer because she had **P**rayed **H**eaven **D**own. By her silent prayer, we learn that a fervent prayer is a heartfelt prayer, but it is not necessarily an audible one.

We are not told that Elkanah saw prayer as the answer. God had given the prayer burden to Hannah and had allowed a most distressing circumstance that she did not choose, did not deserve, and could not change. But, rather than be torn apart, she chose to be "provoked to prayer" as God had desired. Perhaps the adversities you experience in this life will produce the same results when you take it to the Lord in prayer.

Romans 8:28 And we know that all things work together for good to them that love God, to them who are the called according to his purpose.

Those who truly love God will allow Him to work His best in what appears to be adverse situations.

Hannah had made her request known unto God and then went her way in peace. Faith in God can do amazing things. Remember we read that the enemy had provoked her relentlessly year by year. Knowing this gives us a greater appreciation for the release she received by placing her heart-wrenching dilemma in God's hands and leaving it there.

Has God allowed a problem to arise in your life? Are you in a heart-rending circumstance that you did not choose and that you cannot change? If He has allowed the problem, it's because He has planned a glorious solution that will glorify His Son alone.

Because Hannah got down on her knees, she did not remain under the circumstance. We need to do the same. Go to God in prayer. He is concerned about everything that is of concern to you. Through the Blood of His Lamb, we have unlimited access to the One who turns a problem into a great victory when we seek Him.

If you have become frustrated by seemingly unanswered prayers, the Lord wants you to know that it's an honor to be waiting before Him. If you do not enjoy your time of waiting before Him, you will not enjoy most of your lifetime, because most of our lives are spent waiting before Him. He is continually granting your desires while He is working to perfect that which concerns you. Seek to honor Him during your time of waiting.

Just as God had allowed the enemy to provoke Hannah relentlessly year by year, Chapter 2 tells us that she returned year to year to give Samuel a little coat that she had made. And, glory to God, as her life continued, she had three other sons and two daughters. Indeed, God is able to do exceedingly abundantly above all we ask or think. **(Ephesians 3:20)**

Hannah could not read the future chapters of her life and neither can you yours. She had no idea that she would become the mother six children. Like Hannah, we cannot see the paths God has ordained. We are not in a position to understand His determinate counsel. But we can determine to love Him, trust Him, and obey Him.

Hannah, though not mentioned specifically in the New Testament, was greatly honored by God and by Mary, the mother our Lord. Hannah could not have known that her prophetic prayer recorded in **1st Samuel 2:1-10** would be echoed by Mary, the mother of Jesus, and written in **Luke 1:46-55** in what is known as "Mary's Magnificat."

THE CENTURION OF CAPERNAUM

New Testament centurions were Roman officers in command of a hundred soldiers each. Of the seven New Testament centurions referred to, only two are named.

In chapter ten of The Acts of the Apostles, we learn of the glorious conversion of Cornelius the centurion of Caesarea. Later, in Acts 27 we read of Julius the centurion who transported Paul to Rome.

The Capernaum centurion written about in **Luke 7:1-10** remained unnamed. Unlike the account given in Matthew 8, Luke, the storyteller, revealed more of the heart of this unnamed centurion who sought healing for his servant (or slave).

Following His being rejected in Nazareth and the imprisonment of John the Baptist, Matthew 4:13 states that Jesus left Nazareth and that He, " ... came and dwelt at Capernaum," the hometown of five apostles: Peter, Peter's brother Andrew, Matthew, and the brothers James and John. Capernaum was located on the western shore of the Sea of Galilee. It is not named in the Old Testament, but all four New Testament gospels relate details of Jesus' ministry there.

And Capernaum is where we find this unnamed centurion, his sick and "ready to die" servant, and the Son of God. The story related within these ten scriptures provide keen insight into the heart of the unnamed centurion and give clear understanding of true faith in God.

Luke 7:1-2 Now when he had ended all his sayings in the hearing of the people, he entered into Capernaum. And a certain centurion's servant, who was dear unto him, was sick and ready to die.

The term "ready to die" is used three times in scripture and means quite literally what it says. This unnamed servant was going to die had not his master loved him and sought healing on his behalf. It seems certain this unnamed servant was a Jew.

Luke 7:3 And when he heard of Jesus, he sent unto him the elders of the Jews, beseeching him that he would come and heal his servant.

"And when he had heard of Jesus" is not saying that he had only just learned of the Jewish Messiah. All four gospels speak of Jesus being in Capernaum many times prior to this special event. Not knowing if Jesus would respond, the centurion sent Jewish elders to convey the urgency of his request.

The word "beseeching" is used only three times in scripture. The first is in Matthew 8 which relates the same story, and the second is in Mark 1:40 where a leper came kneeling down and beseeching Him. "Beseeching" is an urgent plea from a hopeless, helpless person. The centurion and the Jewish elders knew the servant's situation was both hopeless and helpless aside from God's direct intervention.

Luke 7:4-6 And when they came to Jesus, they besought him earnestly, saying that he was worthy for whom he should do this: for he loveth our nation, and he hath built us a synagogue. Then Jesus went with them...

This situation is indeed curious. The centurion knew, the Jewish elders knew, and Jesus knew, that, if He (Jesus) went into a Gentile's house, He would be considered unclean and defiled. In agreeing to go without hesitancy, was Jesus responding to the need of the servant who was "ready to die," or perhaps to the love expressed through the works done by the centurion on behalf of the Jews? Notice that the elders (and not the centurion himself) were saying the centurion was worthy that He come and heal the servant.

Continuing in verses 6 and 7:
And when he was now not far from the house, the centurion sent friends unto him, saying unto him, Lord, trouble not thyself; for I am not worthy that thou shouldest enter under my roof. Wherefore, neither thought I myself worthy to come unto thee; but say in a word, and my servant shall be healed.

Maybe the centurion had second thoughts about asking Jesus to come into his house and, in so doing, becoming defiled. Notice that this time he sent his friends unto

Jesus. God was creating a circumstance to demonstrate to the centurion, to his friends, to the Jewish elders, and to the "ready to die" servant that He wasn't ready for this man to die but that He was ready to demonstrate who He was and what faith in His word could do!

The centurion continued his request:
Luke 7:8-9 For I also am a man set under authority, having under me soldiers, and I say to one, Go; and he goeth: and to another, Come; and he cometh: and to my servant, Do this; and he doeth it.

The centurion sent friends to express his meek description of his own delegated authority and to recognize that Jesus had God-given authority far above the natural realm. His belief in Jesus' authority was based upon his faith in who Jesus was even though he had not encountered Him personally. Amazing.

We know that Jesus <u>marveled at the unbelief</u> He faced in Nazareth **(Mark 6:6)** and in His own disciples following His resurrection. **(Mark 16:14)** But in the next verse we learn that He <u>marveled at the faith or belief</u> of the Roman centurion.

Luke 7:9-10 When Jesus heard these things, he marveled at him, and turned about, and said unto the people that followed him, *I say unto you, I have not found so <u>great faith</u>, no, not in Israel.* And they that were sent returning to the house, found the servant well that had been sick.

Here Jesus found <u>great faith</u> in the Roman centurion just as He had found <u>great faith</u> in the Syrophenician woman of Canaan. **(Matthew 15:21-28)** Jesus connected acknowledging authority and obedient submission to having "<u>great faith</u>."

In our natural realm, as well as in the spiritual, we must be properly submitted to authority to operate in delegated authority.

The unnamed "sick and ready to die" Jewish slave of a Roman centurion was brought to death's door in order that God would be glorified through the works of His Son.

This story was an actual occurrence. It is not a parable. We can only imagine the impact the servant's healing had upon him, his master, his master's friends, and the Jewish elders.

We, also, can only imagine what this centurion, who loved the Jewish nation and who had built them a synagogue, felt after the Lord was crucified by another Roman centurion who had spit on Him, and bowed on his knees mocking His deity.

THE CRY OF THE LORD

The cry of the Lord is and always has been, "Be ye holy; for I am holy," as **1st Peter 1:16** states in quoting **Leviticus 11:44**.

Proverbs includes these words of wisdom:

Proverbs 16:6 ... by the fear of the Lord men depart from evil.

2nd Corinthians 7:1 Having, therefore, these promises, dearly beloved, let us cleanse ourselves from all filthiness of the flesh and spirit, perfecting holiness in the fear of the Lord.

But this presents a problem. How can feeble, fallen, finite man be perfecting holiness and walk in the fear of the Lord, when, according to:

Isaiah 29:13 ... their fear toward me is taught by the precept (Hebrew word #6673 meaning, "the command") of men ...

After God brought judgment by the flood, He chose to put the fear of man in every beast, fowl of the air, upon all that moved upon the earth and upon all the fish of the sea. **(Genesis 9:2)** However, He desired the "fear of the Lord" to be taught by fathers to their children from generation to generation. **(Deuteronomy 11:19, 32:46)** God chose not to instill the essential "fear of the Lord" into man as He had instilled the fear of man into animals. That's curious.

Today's generation neither knows God nor fears Him. They have not been taught the fear of the Lord; therefore, they do not depart from evil, rather they run to it and then boast of their deeds.

In the first five verses of Proverbs 2: "<u>If thou</u>" is stipulated three times.

Proverbs 2:1-5 My son, <u>if thou</u> wilt receive my words, and hide my commandment with thee, so that thou incline thine ear unto wisdom, and apply thine heart to understanding; yea, <u>if thou</u> cry after knowledge, and lift up thy voice for understanding; <u>if thou</u> seekest her as silver, and searchest for her as for hidden treasures; then thou shalt understand the fear of the Lord, and find knowledge of God.

A key verse for obtaining confidence as we learn to walk in God is found in **Proverbs 28:5**, which says, "… they that seek the Lord understand all things." Those who are earnestly seeking Him will not be misled by the precept of man.

2nd Thessalonians 2:10-12 … with all deceivableness of unrighteousness in them that perish, because they received not the love of the truth, that they might be saved. And for this cause God shall send them strong delusion, that they should believe a lie, that they all might be damned who believed not the truth but had pleasure in unrighteousness.

This scripture does not refer to people who have not been exposed to the truth. It is speaking of those who, when they heard the truth, did not love it enough to depart from all that was unacceptable to God. They did not embrace the love of the truth that they might be saved.

Twelve New Testament scriptures say, "They reasoned among themselves," or "there arose a reasoning among them." All of this "reasoning" of men led to disputes and erroneous conclusions. His counsel to you at this moment is to cease from reasoning among yourselves; do not trust in your own limited understanding. Believers must seek to know and understand Him through His word and by His Spirit.

Let's heed the warning given in **Romans 1:21** which states: "Because when they knew God, they glorified him not as God neither were thankful, but became vain in their imaginations (Greek word #1261 meaning, "reasonings") and their foolish hearts were darkened."

The Book of Isaiah begins with the heart-rending account of God's disappointment in His wayward children.
   Isaiah 1:1-3 Hear, O heavens, and give ear, O earth; for the Lord hath spoken: I have nourished and brought up children, and they have rebelled against me. The ox knoweth his owner, and the ass, his master's crib, but Israel doth not know; my people doth not consider.

This is one of the saddest scriptures in the entire Bible. What an indictment against those who were given opportunity to know and to love their Creator and yet refused. The Lord continued to offer full pardon and reconciliation by pleading in verse 18:

Isaiah 1:18 Come now, and let us reason together, saith the Lord; though your sins be as scarlet; they shall be as white as snow, though they be red like crimson, they shall be as wool.

Genesis is called, "The Book of Origins," or sometimes, "The Book of Beginnings." Some Bible scholars refer to the "Law of First Use" found in Genesis, meaning that generally the "first use" of a term or noun can give a definition that can be traced throughout scripture. This is one of the many things that makes Genesis valuable and interesting. Genesis is where God began His progressive self-revelation, which culminated in Jesus.

Let's go to Genesis 4 where we find Adam and Eve, who became parents of Cain and Abel, after they were disobedient to God. Their sons may have been twins since only one conception is mentioned.

Genesis 4:1-8 And Adam knew Eve his wife, and she conceived, and bore Cain, and said, "I have begotten a man from the Lord." And she again bore his brother, Abel. And Abel was a keeper of sheep, but Cain was a tiller of the ground. And in the process of time it came to pass, that Cain brought forth of the fruit of the ground an offering unto the Lord. And Abel, he also brought of the firstlings of his flock and of the fat thereof. And the Lord had <u>respect</u> unto Abel and to his offering; but unto Cain and unto his offering, he had <u>not respect</u>. And Cain was very wroth (Hebrew #2734 meaning, "to blaze up, of anger, zeal, jealousy"), and his countenance fell. And the Lord said unto Cain, Why art thou wroth (a blaze with anger)? And why is thy countenance fallen? If thou do well, shall thou not be <u>accepted</u>? And if thou do not well, sin lieth at the door. And unto thee shall be his desire, and thou shalt rule over him.

There are many "first use" or "first mention" words in these eight verses. Words such as: conceived, bore, sheep, offering, and others. But, for the purpose of this lesson, we will only focus on two of the first mention words: wroth (anger) and sin.

Verses 6 and 7 contain some of the tenderest words recorded in the entire Bible. Here we find Father God intervening and attempting to <u>reason</u> with Cain <u>before</u> he commits sin. God even goes so far as to express deep concern that his well-being and contentment had been disturbed. Indeed, this is one of the most precious events recorded, and also one of the most tragic. Cain refused God's counsel.

Proverbs 12:15 The way of a fool is right in his own eyes, but he that harkeneth unto counsel is wise.

God asked Cain three questions. There is no record of Cain's verbal response; only his actions. But God doesn't need a verbal response to gauge what is in a man's heart.

1st Samuel 2:3 ... for the Lord is a God of knowledge, and by him actions are weighed.

Actions do speak louder than words. Neither Adam nor Eve honored or feared God even after being told in advance that the consequence of disobedience would bring forth death. **(Genesis 2:17)**

James 1:14-15 But every man is tempted, when he is drawn away of his own lust and enticed. Then when lust hath conceived, it bringeth forth sin; and sin, when it is finished, bringeth forth death.

Note the progression; when the spirit of lust is finished (has done its thing), it results in death.

Cain never experienced the utopian life his parents enjoyed before their disobedience to God. Cain chose to further disobey. His parents did not fear the Lord, and they failed to instill the fear of the Lord in him.

Hebrews 11:4 <u>By faith</u> Abel offered unto God a more excellent sacrifice than Cain ...

Abel's sacrifice offered "by faith" strongly implies a previous instruction in the divinely <u>acceptable</u> way of atoning for sin. Both Cain and Abel had observed their parents' sin being atoned for by blood sacrifice.

Genesis 4:6 contains the first mention of being "wroth" (angry). The point here is not that God was angry with man, as some think and teach, but that man was angry because his own way was <u>not acceptable</u> to God and his brother's was. Anger came from the heart of man; not from the heart of God.

In **4:7** God continued to <u>reason</u> by asking, "If thou do well, shalt thou not be <u>accepted</u>?"

2nd Corinthians 5:9 Wherefore we labor that, whether present or absent, we may be <u>accepted</u> of him.

Isn't it our goal that we might be found <u>acceptable</u> to Him and that we might do well and hear Him say, "Well done, thy good and faithful servant?" **(Matthew 25:23)** My friend, what does it matter what someone else does or doesn't do? All that will matter to you in that day is whether or not He will find your sacrifice to be <u>acceptable</u>.

Cain was not willing to offer a blood sacrifice, and yet he was willing to shed his own brother's blood and then deny knowing anything about it. Why did he think he could lie to God? Why did he have no remorse? Because, my friend, Cain neither feared God nor the consequences of his actions.

Later, he complained after hearing God's judgment against him:
    Genesis 4:13 My punishment is more than I can bear. Behold, thou hast driven me out …

God did not drive Cain from His protection. His own willful sin did. Cain complained that his punishment for willful sin was too great to bear.

Verse 7 contains the first mention of sin and says, "and if thou do not well, sin lieth at the door."

A minister spoke of "sin" as though sin was a person. He substituted the name "Fred" for the word "sin" and read, "If thou do not well, Fred lieth at the door." In his message, he went all through the Bible substituting "Fred" for the word sin. Doing this gave sin a personal identity and made it easy to see that sin is a personal enemy. His message made those who heard acutely aware that they needed to be vigilant and always be watching out for "Fred."

Verse 7 contains another "If," and it's a mighty BIG "If." God offered Cain a free-will choice, and he (Cain) chose to continue in denial. Just as his father Adam before him had denied responsibility and chose instead to blame God by saying, **(Genesis 3:12)** "... the woman whom thou gavest to be with me, she gave me of the tree ..." This is the first recorded "blame shifting" that's so rampant today.

Verse 7, speaking of sin, says, "... and unto thee shall be his desire, and thou shalt rule over him."

These words are close to what God spoke to Eve in **Genesis 3:16**, "... and thy desire shalt be to thy husband, and he shall rule over thee." The difference being that Cain was to rule over sin, all the while sin desired to rule over him. The word "rule" in both scriptures is the same word which means, "to have power, dominion" (Hebrew #4910).

In **Genesis 1:28-29** we learn that man was to subdue the earth and to have dominion, and, yet thousands of years later, we find that weeds (such as marijuana) subdue and have dominion over man. This is strange indeed. We could not even begin to calculate the damage done to man by alcohol made from corn, opium made from poppy seeds, and cocaine made from cocoa leaves. Sadly, weeds, corn, seeds, and leaves have had dominion over many a man and have doomed enumerable souls to hell.

Man does not recognize his true condition. And even "religious man" fails to acknowledge his true condition before Almighty God.

Let's remember and heed the words spoken by Jesus regarding the Laodicean church:
    Revelation 3:17-18 Because thou sayest I am rich, and increased with goods, and have need of nothing, and knowest not that thou art wretched, and miserable, and poor, and blind, and naked, I counsel thee to buy of me gold tried in the fire, that thou mayest be rich; and white raiment, that thou mayest be clothed, and that the shame

of thy nakedness do not appear; and anoint thine eyes with salve, that thou mayest see.

Scripture and experience teach us that God does not change. Just as the Father offered His counsel to Cain, so He offered His counsel to the Laodicean church. The word "wretched is a Greek (#5005) word meaning, "miserable." Webster's Dictionary adds: "contemptible, despicable, very inferior, of base character." Truly, the "religious man," in his carnal state, does not recognize his wretched condition before God. Like Cain, he chooses to remain in denial.

Adam and Eve disobeyed and then attempted to "hide themselves," but this was not the case with Cain. Did Cain murder his brother out behind the barn or off in the woods? No, Cain murdered his brother in an open field, and then denied knowing anything about it. And this he did after Father God graciously and lovingly attempted to reason with him.

Cain could have obtained mercy and have been a recipient of compassionate love. How do we know this? We know it by studying God's Word.

Psalm 103:13 As a father <u>pitieth</u> his children, so the Lord <u>pitieth</u> them that <u>fear him</u>.

This word "pitieth" (Hebrew #7355) means "to love, especially compassionately, to find or obtain mercy." So, especially compassionate love and mercy are extended to "them that fear him." God desires for His especially compassionate love to continue through the generations.

Luke 1:50 And his mercy is on them that <u>fear him</u> from generation to generation.

Psalm 147:11 The Lord taketh pleasure in those who <u>fear him</u>, in those who hope in his mercy.

1st Peter 1:17 And <u>if</u> ye call on the Father who without <u>respect</u> of persons judgeth according to every man's work, <u>pass the time of your sojourning here in fear</u> ...

Notice the words <u>respect</u> and <u>fear</u>, and remember that God had <u>respect</u> unto Abel's offering. His offering was evidence that he feared and reverenced God.

Malachi 3:16-17 Then they that <u>feared</u> the Lord spoke often one to another; and the Lord harkened, and heard it, and a book of remembrance was written before him for them that <u>feared</u> the Lord, and that thought upon his name. And they shall be mine, saith the Lord of hosts, in that day when I make up my jewels; and I will spare them, as a man spareth his own son that serveth him.

What is the Lord saying to us by these scriptures? First, His desire is, "... be ye holy; for I am holy." **(1st Peter 1:16)** In other words, "Be as I am." One reason God created man was to have fellowship with him throughout eternity. To have fellowship with God, we must be holy.

Hebrews 12:14 ... without which (referring to holiness) no man shall see the Lord.

And don't you want to see Him? Don't you want to look upon His face?

We read that we are to be perfecting holiness in the fear of the Lord but also that the fear of the Lord can be taught by the precept of man.

Clay Roberts is the son of a man who preached years ago. He has said that his father preached that anyone who drove a two-toned car or a car with whitewall tires was going to hell. Was this preacher leading lambs into the love of the truth? Was he teaching according to true understanding of God and His word?

Clay rebelled before reaching manhood and "threw out the baby with the bath water," so to speak. He rejected the word of God and turned to the temporal pleasures of this life. He came to his lowest point as he sat with a buddy in the woods one day. While shooting up heroin, he turned to his friend and boasted, "I'll see you in hell."

Fortunately for him, God had other plans. This son of the misinformed preacher is a preacher himself today who pastor's a flock of lambs by teaching them the true fear of the Lord.

We recently heard a man say that a short-sleeved shirt could send a man to hell and that a man's wedding band could accomplish the same thing.

Are examples like these what God spoke through **Isaiah in 29:13**, "... their fear toward me is taught by the precept of man?"

Some religious leaders today, like the Pharisees of old, rather than leading lambs into the glorious liberty of Jesus, lead them into bondage and confusion. Who can have confidence in God when worried that his salvation hinges on the length of his shirtsleeves or on driving a two-toned car?

God, in speaking to Job's friends, said, **(Job 42:8)** "... and my servant Job will pray for you; for him will I <u>accept</u>."

Remember God told Cain before he committed murder, "If ye <u>do well</u>, ye will be <u>accepted</u>."

1st Peter 2:20 But if ye <u>do well</u> and suffer for it, ye take it patiently, this is <u>acceptable</u> with God.

Isaiah 1:16-17 Wash yourselves, make yourselves clean; put away the evil of your doings from before mine eyes; cease to do evil; learn to <u>do well</u>.

Acts 10:34-35 Then Peter opened his mouth (speaking to the Gentile household of Cornelius), and said, Of a truth I perceive that God is no <u>respecter</u> of persons; but in every nation he that feareth him, and worketh righteousness, is <u>accepted</u> by him.

For the purpose of this study, the key words are: respecter, feareth, and accepted. Earlier, in Genesis, we learned that God had no respect unto Cain or his offering, but that He had respect for Abel and his offering.

After being privately counseled by Father God, Cain's actions demonstrated that he did not fear God.

It is vital that we understand that, whereas God is no respecter of persons, he most assuredly is a respecter of sacrifices.

Ephesians 1:6 He (by His Blood sacrifice) hath made us accepted in the beloved.

Romans 12:1 I beseech you therefore, brethren, by the mercies of God, that ye present your bodies a living sacrifice, holy, acceptable unto God, which is your reasonable service.

Has your fear of the Lord been taught by the precept of man or upon God's standard learned by knowing and understanding Him through His Spirit and by His word?

God desires to be pleased with His people. Walk in the true fear of the Lord; for His counsel to you is, "Be ye holy; for I am holy."

THE DEAD ARE TO BE BURIED
An interesting Biblical perspective

Scriptures teach that the dead are to be buried, except when death occurs as a judgment of God.

God instructed His people to bury the dead (including enemies killed in battle) as soon as possible in order that the land not be defiled (polluted). **Deuteronomy 21:23, 1st Kings 11:15**

In some instances, He instructed them NOT to bury the dead as a show of divine judgment:
Jeremiah 14:16, 16:4-6, 25:33

In a vivid display of divine judgment upon idolatrous Israel, God said:
Ezekiel 6:5 And I will lay the dead carcasses of the children of Israel before their idols; and I will scatter your bones round about your altars.

The thirty-ninth chapter of Ezekiel uses the term, "cleanse the land" when referring to burying the dead.

Ezekiel 39:12-13 And seven months shall the house of Israel be burying them, that they may cleanse the land.

Indication that Joseph's brothers hated their father Jacob is evidenced by them having him believe Joseph was devoured by wild beasts, and; thus, no body was left to bury. Having no body to bury was an ultimate defilement for the people of God. Therefore, Jacob's grief was greatly intensified.

Genesis 49:29 records the dying Jacob stating his own burial desires. And Genesis 50: concludes with Joseph's death. In verse 25 it is written, "And Joseph took an oath of the children of Israel, saying, God will surely visit you, and ye shall carry up my bones from here."

Joshua honored Joseph's wishes 179 years later:

Joshua 24:32 And the bones of Joseph, which the children of Israel brought up out of Egypt, buried they in Shechem ...

In the matter of Jezebel, wife of Ahab, whose name has become synonymous with "wicked woman," we can only say that the judgment of God made an utter end of her.

God spoke through Elijah the prophet, who instructed a young man to anoint Jehu as king over Israel and to say that he was to "smite the house of Ahab." **(2ⁿᵈ Kings 9:6)** The young man did as he was told and spoke these words before witnesses:

2ⁿᵈ Kings 9:10 And the dogs shall eat Jezebel in the portion of Jezreel, and then there shall be none to bury her.

Ahab was the first king of Israel to be allied by marriage to a heathen princess. His wife, Jezebel was passionately devoted to the debased sensual worship of strange gods.

When Jehu came to Jezreel, Jezebel heard about it and painted her face, covered her head, and looked down out a window. Jehu looked up to the window and called to her eunuchs asking whose side they were on. The eunuchs then made a swift decision as to whose side they were on and threw her out the window to her death. **(2nd Kings 9:30-32)**

2nd Kings 9:33 And he said, Throw her down. So they threw her down: and some of her blood was sprinkled on the wall, and on the horses; and he trod her under foot.

Jehu then enjoyed a hearty meal before instructing his men, "Go, see now this cursed woman, and bury her; for she is a king's daughter." **(2nd Kings 9:34)**

2nd Kings 9:35-37 And they went to bury her; but they found no more than her skull, and the feet, and the palms of her hands. Wherefore they came again, and told him. And he said, This is the word of the Lord, which he spoke by his servant Elijah the Tishbite, saying, In the portion of Jezreel shall dogs eat the flesh of Jezebel; and the carcass of Jezebel shall be as dung upon the face of the field in the portion of Jezreel, so that they not say, This is Jezebel.

God ordained that no grave be made to commemorate Jezebel's life or death. The blood of Ahab, her husband, was also licked up by dogs following his death. **(Kings 22:38)**

NOTE: Dogs spoken of in scripture were not the domesticated household pets of today. They were feral (ferocious, savage) dogs that roamed in search of food wherever it could be found.

(More concerning burying of the dead)

THE INFAMOUS MADALYN MURRAY O'HAIR
Was her death and non-burial a judgment of God?

On September 29, 1995, the earthly life of the infamous Madalyn Murray O'Hair ended. Her vain search for significance ended when she met her death on a Texas ranch at the hands of her former office manager and ex-con, David Waters, who fulfilled his fantasy of gruesomely torturing her.

Wikipedia reports that Madalyn Murray O'Hair was the voice and face of atheism in America during the 1960's and 1970's after she succeeded in a 1963 lawsuit ending Bible reading in American public schools. The U.S. Supreme Court, in an 8-1 decision, voted in her favor thus catapulting her into the infamy she relished. A previous lawsuit won the prior year put an end to prayer in U.S. public schools.

Loving to bask in the notoriety spotlight, Madalyn enjoyed television and magazine interviews. She was quoted in a 1965 Playboy Magazine interview as saying religion was, "a crutch, an irrational reliance on superstition, and a supernatural nonsense."

She was the founder of the American Atheists organization, which empowered radical non-believers to voice their beliefs.

Here is a quote of Madalyn O'Hair's core beliefs:

There is no god. There is no hell. There are no angels. When you die, you go in the ground, and the worms eat you. No god ever gave man anything, never answered any prayer at any time, nor will ever.

In January 2001, David Waters confessed to her murder and led police to the ranch where he had tortured and extensively mutilated Madalyn, John Murray her son, and granddaughter Robin Murray six years before. Their bodies had been sawed in dozens of pieces. DNA tests revealed the identities of Jon and Robin. <u>However; all that was left to identify the seventy-six-year-old Madalyn was the serial number on her prosthetic hip</u>.

William J. Murray, Madalyn's son, revealed that her entire life was engulfed in the love of power. He stated that her life's central theme was her pursuit of center stage and control. He reported that his mother spent days in theaters watching pornographic movies alone although she was the only woman in the audience.

In his autobiographical book, "My Life Without God," William J. Murray detailed the consuming hatred of his mother toward God. William J. Murray became a Christian 1980 and is the founder and president of the Religious Freedom Coalition.

QUESTION: Was Madalyn Murray O'Hair's death and non-burial the result of the judgment of God?

 **THIRTY AND EIGHT YEARS**

(Scriptures are from the Gospel of John unless noted)

There are intriguing similarities between the Israelites' thirty-eight year delay in entering the Promised Land and the thirty and eight years of misery experienced by the unnamed infirm man at the pool of Bethesda. Some of these will be considered at the conclusion of our study.

Chapter 5 of the **Gospel of John** begins the outward opposition to Jesus by the religious crowd who had zeal without true knowledge of God. The hostility increased until Jesus was totally rejected by the religious authorities in Chapter 7.

5:1-2 After this there was a feast of the Jews, and Jesus went up to Jerusalem. Now there is at Jerusalem, by the sheep gate, a pool, which is called in the Hebrew tongue Bethesda, having five porches.

The present-day Muslim quarter of Jerusalem encompasses the pool of Bethesda site where an Islamic inscription has been over its entryway from the time it became a Muslim theological school.

Extensive excavations reveal the pool to be 160' by 480' with a depth of 45'. Bethesda is a Greek word (#964) meaning, "house of kindness" and is only mentioned here in the Bible. Jesus bestowed extraordinary kindness upon an ungrateful man there.

5:3-4 In these lay a great multitude of impotent folk, of blind, lame, paralyzed, waiting for the moving of the water. For an angel went down at a certain season into the pool, and troubled the water; whosoever then first, after the troubling of the water, stepped in was made whole (well) of whatever disease he had.

The Greek (#770) word "impotent" means "to be feeble, weak, or diseased."

5:5-6 And a certain man was there, who had an infirmity thirty and eight years. When Jesus saw him lie there, and knew that he had been thus now a long time, he saith unto him, Wilt thou be made whole (well)?

The meaning of the Greek (#769) word "infirmity" is similar to the word "impotent." It means "frail, feeble in body or mind." Notice that the scripture says this man had had an infirmity thirty and eight years. We are not told how long he had been at the pool Bethesda, but, we can appreciate that he experienced prolonged disappointment and had little hope of his life's circumstance becoming even tolerable.

Jesus, knowing he had been there a long time asked, "Wilt thou be made whole?" We might expect his predictable answer would have been, "Yes, I need to be made whole. Master, have mercy on me and heal me!" But that never happened.

5:7 The impotent man answered him, Sir, I have no man, when the water is troubled, to put me into the pool; but while I am coming, another steppeth down before me.

It's interesting that this man never asked to be healed. Instead, he complained of how he was treated by others. It's also interesting that Jesus disregarded his complaint. And, like the woman at the well and the nobleman of Capernaum, this unnamed infirm man only addressed Jesus as, "Sir."

Being acutely aware of his own hopeless dilemma may have diminished his perception of who it was that spoken to him. It may have been that Jesus was asking, "Do you want to be healed or do you want to continue whining while wallowing in self-pity?"

5:8-9 Jesus saith unto him, Rise, take up thy bed, and walk. And immediately the man was made whole, and took up his bed, and walked; and the same day was the Sabbath.
Jesus did not require this man to have faith to be healed. Even with knowing the cause of the man's infirmity was sin, Jesus mercifully chose to relieve his suffering. We aren't told that this man ever expressed gratitude for

Jesus speaking a few words that ended his thirty and eight years of misery. Note that he was healed (restored) instantaneously without needing an extensive stay in a rehabilitation center.

Jesus <u>did not</u> say, "Take up thy bed and follow <u>me</u>." Eighteen scriptures record Him encouraging others to, "Follow me," but these words were not spoken to this man. Hmmm.

This man and his condition were well known amongst the people of Jerusalem. Oddly, we are not told that anyone rejoiced over his healing. His healing was the turning point that marked the beginning of the sharp decline in Jesus' acceptability with the Jews.

5:10-13 The Jews, therefore, said unto him that was cured, It is the Sabbath day; it is not lawful for thee to carry thy bed. He answered them, he that made me whole the same said unto me, Take up thy bed and walk. Then they asked him, What man is that who said unto thee, Take up thy bed and walk? And he that was healed knew not who it was; for Jesus had moved away, a multitude being in that place.

It's as though he was saying, "Hey, I didn't do anything wrong. I'm not at fault here. I just did what I was told. And don't forget, I never asked to be healed."

In the Jewish religious mindset, Jesus had sinned for healing this man on the Sabbath.

5:14 Afterward Jesus findeth him in the temple, and said unto him, Behold, thou art made whole; <u>sin no more</u>, lest a worse thing come unto thee.

Notice that Jesus <u>found</u> him in the temple. The healed man was not looking for Jesus, but Jesus was looking for him to warn him of something he knew already. His thirty and eight years of infirmity had been caused by sin.

Scripture records at least three types of sickness: sickness unto death, sickness unto chastisement, and sickness unto the glory of God.

Perhaps Jesus chose this man among the great multitude at the pool in order to create a platform to openly declare who He was, as He did in the remaining twenty-nine verses of this chapter.

The ungrateful healed man's heart reaction became an action that was recorded in the next verse.

5:15 The man departed, and told the Jews that it was Jesus who made him well.

Jesus had sought him, but he sought the Jewish authorities to tattle. What did his actions say about his heart? Yes, he did take up his bed and walk. He walked directly to the religious authorities. Certainly, he was aware of the smoldering tumult concerning Jesus. He knew, too, that his being healed would fuel their outrage.

He had been told, "Sin no more, lest a worse thing come unto thee."

Here are two questions to ponder: Did he sin no more? Did a worse thing come unto him?

5:16 And therefore did the Jews persecute Jesus, and sought to slay him, because he had done these things on the Sabbath day.

No one glorified God. Their hearts remained blinded by vain traditions.

5:17-18 But Jesus answered them, my Father worketh hitherto, and I work. Therefore, the Jews sought the more to kill him, because he not only had broken the Sabbath, but said also that God was his Father, making himself equal with God.

In classic cannonball candor, Jesus got to the crux of the matter. He added insult to injury by declaring that God was His Father. Often wrong but never in doubt, the Jews who heard His words were aghast that a mere mortal man would claim to be equal to God.

The many man-made amendments to the Law of Moses prevented the common people from truly loving God in simplistic sincerity, as He desired.

Mark 12:37 ... And the common people heard him gladly.

Lord, grant that we be common people who gladly hear Your voice and who know You.

By doing the works of the Father, Jesus effectively defrocked their cloak of pious hypocrisy. He healed a man with a paralyzed hand in the synagogue on a Sabbath day. **(Matthew 12:9-14)** He healed a man of dropsy in a Pharisee's house on another Sabbath day. **(Luke 14:1-6)** Neither of these men asked to be healed. We are not told that they were grateful or that they then followed Jesus.

The remaining twenty-seven verses of chapter 5 of the **Gospel of John** contain only the words of Jesus in which he spoke of "the Son" seven times and "the Father" twelve. Identifying God as "the Father" was something new for the Jews. And here, Jesus spoke of God as being "the Father" and of Himself as being, "the Son." It would be an incredible understatement to say that those listening were incensed by such declarations.

Remember that the article, "the" is singular. Using a capitol "F" in Father and a capitol "S" for son makes them proper nouns: a specific title or name. Jesus declared that He was <u>the Son of the Father</u>.

ANOTHER THIRTY AND EIGHT YEARS

The thirty and eight year time span experienced by the infirm man is curious. It may relate to the one other thirty and eight year time period the Bible records.

After they rebelled and were defeated by the Amorites, scripture begins to record God's reasoning and direction for His chosen ones.

Deuteronomy 1:45-46 And ye returned and wept before the Lord; but the Lord would not hearken to your voice, nor give ear unto you. So ye abode in Kadesh many days, according unto the days that ye abode there.

Deuteronomy 2:14-18 And the period in which we came from Kadesh-barnea, until we were come over the brook Zered, was <u>thirty and eight years</u>, until all the generation of the men of war were perished from among the host, as the Lord swore unto them. For indeed the hand of the Lord was against them, to destroy them from among the host, until they were consumed. So it came to pass, when all the men of war were consumed and dead from among the people, That the Lord spoke unto me, saying, Thou art to pass over through ...

Their thirty and eight year delay ended as they began to move toward their appointed destiny: conquering the land of Canaan. Their **GPS** kicked in once **G**od's **P**urposes were **S**erved, and the first generation of Israelites then moved ahead.

Miriam had died at Kadesh. Aaron had died on Mt. Hur. Moses was to die on Mt. Nebo in the land of Moab. Though he was 120 years old, his eyes were not dim, nor his natural force abated. **Deuteronomy 34:7**

Spotting similarities between the only two specific thirty- and eight year time spans mentioned in the Bible is interesting. Here are some:

ISRAEL'S THIRTY AND EIGHT YEAR JOURNEY

- ❖ Invalid Israel blamed others for their predicament.

- ❖ They were impotent because they failed to believe both God and Moses.

- ❖ Ungrateful Israelites lacked the courage to defeat their enemies.

- ❖ After thirty-eight years, during which all who had come out of Egypt had died, only first generation Israelites entered the Promise Land.

THE IMPOTENT MAN'S THIRTY AND EIGHT YEAR WAIT

- ❖ The invalid man blamed others for his predicament.

- ❖ The impotent man was not grateful.

- ❖ When healed, he lacked the courage to walk with Jesus.

- ❖ The ungrateful man languished thirty-eight years without being aware of his true need.

Jesus quoted the prophet Isaiah when speaking at the synagogue in His hometown of Nazareth:

Luke 4:18-21 The Spirit of the Lord is upon me, because he hath anointed me to preach the gospel to the poor; he hath sent me to heal the brokenhearted, to preach deliverance to the captives, and recovering of sight to the blind, to set at liberty them that are bruised, to preach the acceptable year of the Lord. And he closed the book, and he gave it again to the minister, and sat down. And the eyes of all them that were in the synagogue were fastened on him. And he began to say unto them, This day is this scripture fulfilled in your ears.

Perhaps this scripture would have been fulfilled in the impotent man personally had he recognized his sin, forsaken it, and followed Jesus.